Voices, Choices AND Second Chances

How to Win the Battle to Bring Opportunity Scholarships to Your State

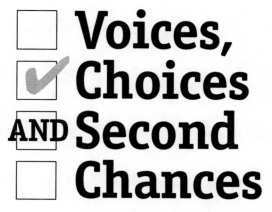

Voices, Choices
AND Second
Chances

How to Win the Battle to Bring Opportunity Scholarships to Your State

*Based on the Dramatic Story
and Ultimately Successful Campaign
of D.C. Parents for School Choice*

Virginia Walden Ford

D.C. Parents for School Choice

WASHINGTON ★ D.C.

Contents

"The school choice movement should become the second American Revolution."

Eugene Hickok
Under Secretary of Education
U.S. Department of Education
August 2002

Foreword

Virginia Walden Ford is a warrior. She is unafraid and utterly committed to empowering parents to be able to make the best decisions possible for the education of their children. Her courage, her steadfastness, and her dedication all make her a powerful force in the parental choice movement.

Virginia and I first met when we were both invited to testify at a Senate hearing sometime in the late nineties. We became friends and colleagues in the battle for parental choice. In 1999, Virginia became one of the founders of the Black Alliance for Educational Options (BAEO), which is a national, nonprofit membership organization whose mission is to actively support parental choice to empower families and increase quality educational options for black children.

I've been working closely with her ever since, and I've been able to see firsthand her influence in this movement and how deeply it affects her. Some of what has happened as part of her particular fight in D.C. has been rough for her, but publicly she does not buckle. It sometimes breaks her heart, but never her spirit. She carefully considers her actions, and when she believes she is doing what's right for the parents and children, she is undaunted in the face of controversy and criticism.

I know that Virginia is always trying to help others learn from her experience. She is interested in passing on her "lessons learned" in a way that truly connects with people and helps them embrace their own power. In this book, Virginia accomplishes that mission.

Howard L. Fuller, Ph.D.
Former Superintendent of Milwaukee Public Schools
Distinguished Professor of Education and
Founder/Director of the Institute for the
Transformation of Learning at
Marquette University

Introduction

"Several years ago, I was a single mother with a son in ninth grade. When my son started having problems in and out of school, I knew I did not want him to continue attending Roosevelt High School, a D.C. public school that had (and still has) many problems of its own.

"Thanks to a neighbor's financial help, I was able to send my son to a private high school, where his grades and attitude immediately began to improve. He has now graduated and is serving in the U.S. Marine Corps and doing very well. I still shudder to think how very different his life would have been had he not been able to attend a school that offered a strong academic program and an environment that inspired him to succeed."

From the testimony of Virginia Walden Ford, Committee on Education in the Workforce Hearings, April 16, 2001

My son William was about eleven years old when one of his friends was beaten so severely that he wound up paralyzed. During the assault, the boy's attackers repeatedly yelled at him, "You think you're so damn smart? You ain't smart!"

That was the beginning of trouble for William. Thereafter, his grades began to slide. He soon started mouthing off, skipping school, and hanging out with a bad crowd. He told me that he just didn't feel safe anymore, and the reason he'd taken up with some thugs was to protect himself from others like them.

By the time he was a freshman in high school, William was getting in hot water with the police. One afternoon, after about a dozen suspensions from school, he came home with another one. That evening, I sat on our front porch, desperately trying to figure out what I was going to do to help this child.

A neighbor of ours, Bob Lewis, came by and asked what was wrong. When I told him that my youngest was in trouble again, he encouraged me, "We have got to find a way to save William. He deserves saving for his sake, as well as for yours."

We'd met only once before, and I didn't know Bob well. The man told me that he saw something special in my son, and he would do everything in his power to help. His compassion was obviously deep and sincere, and I took some comfort from this: William would benefit from any time or attention Bob could give him. I imagined he would be a good role model and mentor. Bob had grown up in our neighborhood and gone away to college, then returned with his wife when they were starting a family.

Just a week later, Bob came to our house and surprised us with a check. "We're going to enroll William in the school I attended," he told me. Both William and I were stunned by this selfless act of generosity. Bob took us to Archbishop Carroll, a parochial school nearby, introduced us to the faculty and administration, then helped us with the paperwork, and he has never asked for anything in return.

Right away, William's behavior changed. In the first week, he began engaging with his teachers, caring about his schoolwork, and doing well. Quickly, he learned that he wasn't just funny (he'd always been a clown), but he could also excel athletically and academically. When I asked him why things were so drastically different, he told me, "Mama, I feel like people at this school care about me. Before, the only person who cared whether I learned or not was you. Now it seems like a lot of people care. Most of all, I feel safe."

William spent two years at Archbishop Carroll, and then I moved him to a charter school for his senior year. By then, he had gained the confidence he needed to attend a public school again. William graduated first in his class.

Many of my son's old friends were not so lucky. It's sad how many have fallen into the world of drugs or wound up in jail. As you might expect, some of them are no longer alive. If only they'd had the same chances as William did.

Real Choices Right Now

Clearly, William had potential, but because of the trouble he was in, it was hard for anyone to see it. This happens often with poor kids: They react and respond negatively to their environment, they get labeled "at-risk," and the system isn't set up to help them make a change and begin to thrive.

School choice promises a different result. It makes options available so children who would otherwise get lost in the system can be given the chance to have what everyone else takes for granted: a good quality educational environment.

This book is not about what's wrong with public schools, or even how to solve the problems that plague the students, faculty, and administration in this struggling institution. Instead, it's about finding a solution for parents who know that waiting until the system is fixed will not address the needs of their children now. This book teaches parents how to fight to free children and their families from failing schools. It will equip them to speak out and ultimately provide choice so that the right environment can be given to each child.

Although I have been in the school choice movement for many years, William's success truly brings home the power of scholarships to me. Yet my experience is not unique. This book includes many moving stories of parents who were able to make a difference for children who were struggling or worse. It will give you *instructions* for running a school choice campaign, and it will also provide you with *inspiration* to help you stay the course when you're disheartened, disappointed, or simply tired. Believe me, you'll need both.

I'm the first to admit that this work can be exhausting. The many people who have passionately lobbied for the voucher program in Washington, D.C., can attest to that with me. We all worked together, both when we were fired up and when it felt like someone had thrown a wet blanket on the whole affair. It takes the proverbial tireless dedication to get legislation passed to provide parents with the choices they need and to give children the chances they deserve.

The Basic Model for Private Scholarship Programs

Most of the opportunity scholarship/voucher programs that exist in the United States today follow a basic model. In general, a privately funded trust or foundation implements school choice through a voucher program based on the following:

✓ Children are eligible whose families meet financial requirements. Usually, the conditions follow the Federal Free or Reduced Price School Lunch Program guidelines.

✓ Students must stay in school, and parents must pay a portion of the tuition.

Where We've Been

The school choice movement began in the 1980s and really started to heat up in the '90s, when the Milwaukee Parental Choice Program was established. It was challenged in court but ultimately upheld. By 2004, that program had grown from 341 to nearly 15,000 students and expanded to include some religious schools. Along the way, the nation's teachers' unions, the National Association for the Advancement of Colored People (NAACP), and the American Civil Liberties Union (ACLU) started to oppose it loudly, arguing that vouchers undermine public school systems by diverting funds and defy the constitutional separation of church and state by putting public dollars into religious schools.

Each of those issues has been addressed in various venues, including the ultimate authority, the Supreme Court. In a landmark case in 2002, the Supreme Court justices upheld the constitutionality of vouchers in Cleveland, and education reformers across the nation breathed a sigh of relief: Opportunity scholarships would continue to be a viable option for many states in the nation.

Unfortunately, more than thirty U.S. states are held back by amendments that restrict the use of state funds in private schools, thereby prohibiting opportunity scholarships. Named after House Speaker James G. Blaine who proposed such an amendment in 1875, these so-called Blaine amendments can be changed, and this book will help you do it. In states where this obstacle doesn't exist, and the desire for school choice does, we're poised to give you all the resources you need, except your own personal voice and story.

Where We're Headed

Not long before the Supreme Court case, President Clinton had vetoed a bill that our group, D.C. Parents for School Choice, as well as the Center for Education Reform and the National Center for Neighborhood Enterprise, had lobbied long and hard to get through both houses of Congress. It was a painful loss but, as they say, we went on to fight another day. Between that defeat and our ultimate success in early 2004, we were on a roller-coaster ride of tremendous support, surprising betrayals, and hard-won victories.

The triumphant efforts of D.C. Parents for School Choice, along with the pioneering successes in such states as Wisconsin and Ohio, convince me that *you can do this* if you are committed and surround yourself with other parents who are as dedicated to the cause as you are.

This fight can be noble, uplifting, and incredibly rewarding. In this book, I'll use the story of our campaign to help you foresee potential pitfalls, as well as capitalize on what we learned that really works. You'll get . . .

- ✓ the background you need to speak convincingly about the success of voucher-program students across the United States;
- ✓ help in developing your media messages plus the basic templates for getting those messages heard;
- ✓ strategies for rallying your grassroots support and empowering fellow parents to become influential public speakers;
- ✓ ideas on fundraising and securing financial support;
- ✓ tips for running an effective, volunteer-based organization;
- ✓ tactics for dealing with political attacks; and
- ✓ encouragement for staying the course.

Clearly, our opponents are just as serious in their convictions as we are. That's why it's so important to fully mobilize parents and community leaders and to effectively solicit both political and financial backing. You will need to learn to work with the media, seek the counsel of seasoned publicists, and graciously accept both attack and defeat—and to persist anyway. Working with politicians can be both thrilling and challenging, but as long as you keep the students foremost in your mind, school choice can be a reality for you and the children who most need your help.

1

Build Organizational Leadership: Finding Parents with Passion

"Wherever we find mediocrity, this society has an obligation to challenge that. And that's what we're talking about today. We're talking about making sure no child gets left behind by focusing on each child. And the best way to focus on each child is to look at results and then remember who the decision-maker is in society. The decision-maker is the mom or the dad."
From the remarks of President George W. Bush, addressed to Kipp D.C. Key Academy in Washington, D.C., July 1, 2003

As I walked out the door on my way to meet a busload of parents who were revved up and ready to attend a rally, one of our organizers took me aside and reported, "Virginia, we raised the bail money, so you can stop worrying about it."

She knew I'd been fretting because we were going to be demonstrating without a permit, which could stir up some legal problems for our members. The cash was some comfort, though it didn't totally calm my nerves. Who wants to tangle with the police? Nobody, and especially not single parents who have just managed to cram one more "to do" into their already incredibly busy lives.

We boarded the bus, and once we were on the road, I turned to these people, our front line, and said, "Look, this is serious. We could be arrested today, because we don't have a permit. If you don't want to participate fully, I understand. But we do have bail money, and—"

Before I could get the rest of it out, they all started talking at once. "I can go to jail," one would say to her friend, "but you'll need to pick up my kids this afternoon, so don't get yourself arrested. Who else is in that part of town? Okay, they can all go over to my mother's for the night, if need be." They immediately started figuring out how they could help one another and still finish the job they'd committed to do.

Every grassroots organization should be graced with the kind of people who participate in D.C. Parents for School Choice. Their dedication never fails to impress me, and their constant willingness to do whatever it takes has always impressed upon me how critical they are to the effectiveness of our campaign. A successful volunteer-based organization requires that every person involved have this kind of dedication. In particular, it starts with the leadership—the parent organizers—and this chapter will give you a clear plan for finding and developing those leaders, whether you are establishing a relatively small group in your community or organizing a statewide, or even nationwide, network of parent groups.

Incidentally, no one was arrested on that day or any other one. We had spent so much time on Capitol Hill that the security police knew us. They'd seen us come day after day in our D.C. Parents for School Choice T-shirts, sometimes with our children. We frequently met in front of the Capitol to eat, regroup, or get assignments to go to other buildings.

The day of this particular rally, the police told us we had to leave because there were too many of us blocking the entrance to the Rayburn Building. We had come to participate in a hearing the opposition had scheduled, and we'd arrived early. The head officer pulled me aside to tell me we had to leave, but he asked me just how long we intended to be there, and I told him we'd be leaving to go to the hearing shortly. He smiled and told me how he had watched us over the months and how much he admired our persistence and passion. He'd have to report us, he said, but it might take him a while to get through to the office, so we might be gone by the time he got back, right? I smiled in gratitude for the warning and made sure we were gone before he returned.

Where to Begin

Because you're reading this book now, I know you're someone who believes in the power of one person to make a difference. And if you're like me, you recognize that although you may have some useful skills, you'll need the help of other people who are willing to stick their necks out, too, to accomplish something significant.

In forming a grassroots organization, you'll be creating a powerful agent for change. To be successful, your group must involve committed people who are risk takers willing to fight for what they want. This means that your most powerful allies will be those who have a personal stake in establishing a school choice program in your area.

Should your organization be formally up and running before you start recruiting parents to join you in leadership? Not necessarily. The success of your campaign depends far more on the commitment and quality of the parents involved, and you can start building your network right away. Getting to know the community can happen long before you get your nonprofit status or any financial backing. Not that those things are unimportant—and they will be addressed later—but truly, your parent leaders are the key to your success, so let's start with them.

You may already have a group of people who are working with you. Then again, you may be the only one you know who's championing the cause in your area right now. Either way, this chapter should help you expand your core leadership.

How will you find and train everyone? It's not terribly difficult, though it will require a sizable investment of time.

Below are the steps I implemented in recruiting and developing people for D.C. Parents for School Choice. Anyone can follow them to institute a similar campaign.

1. *Become visible in the community.* Volunteer to help with community projects; tell people about your commitment to school choice and share your personal story; and get to know the neighborhood heroes, those people on whom the community relies and trusts.

2. *Identify and invite those who will be good advocates for the cause.* Consider everyone you meet, plus consult your neighborhood heroes to tell you who will be most eager to participate.

3. *Remind them that they have the right to speak out.* Help them find their own voices and learn to tell their unique stories.

4. *Stay in regular contact and let them know they are vital to the campaign.* Be sure your parent leaders remain enthusiastic and feel supported in their efforts.

Step 1. Become Visible in the Community

Back in the late nineties, I was the community outreach coordinator for a group called FOCUS (Friends of Choice in Urban Schools) when it became crystal clear that we needed a parent organization to support the growing charter school movement in the District of Columbia. Because I had some experience with organizing parents, I decided to get the ball rolling. This was my personal training ground for what would later become the D.C. Parents for School Choice campaign. What I learned then can be used in any grassroots effort, and we applied it successfully to get the voucher program established in Washington, D.C.

My first order of business, as it should be for you, was simply to become identifiable in the community. In other words, I went into all the neighborhoods that would be affected by a school choice program in the District and participated in meetings, from city commissions to Boys and Girls Club gatherings, and volunteered to help out whenever their needs dovetailed with my interests. I made a special effort to attend anything to do with children's education, but I also spent many evenings just going wherever people were discussing community issues.

Doing this has two main benefits. First, you become intimately acquainted with what's important to the people in your area. Second, they get to know you as a serious contributor to your community.

While this activity is crucial, it's not enough by itself. To discover likely candidates to help you lead the campaign, you must find your way to the community's heart. One of the most important things I did, both in gaining people's trust and determining who would be passionate parent organizers, was to seek out and get to know the neighborhood heroes. If you've ever lived in a community with a lot of single parents, you know who I'm talking about. There's always someone who takes care of everyone else—one lady who babysits for next to nothing and who will feed your kids if you're late getting home from work, usually from a second job. That's the kind of person you are seeking. If you can endear yourself to her, you cement your relationship with the community. She is also your single greatest source of information about who will be eager to work with you, who will follow through on commitments, and who will have the influence and energy to bring other parents to the table, too.

Step 2. Identify and Invite Those Who Will Be Good Advocates for the Cause

As you work with others in your community and get to know people who share your concerns about the quality of education for all children, some of them will shine as superstars. Others may take a little coaxing and coaching to fully come into their own.

Consider this list, developed by my colleagues, Ron Harris and Donna Watson of Children First America, a school choice advocacy group in Austin, Texas. Following are the characteristics they identify as important for a grassroots leader to possess:

- ✓ Passionate about school choice
- ✓ Has a compelling story to tell or can identify with other parents' stories
- ✓ Knowledgeable about school choice and sees the "bigger picture"
- ✓ Is honest; has integrity
- ✓ Articulate spokesperson, able to speak well and persuasively
- ✓ Presents self well in front of one or many
- ✓ A good organizer, can put together a successful meeting
- ✓ Has the capacity to rally the troops
- ✓ Likes people, has the ability to listen, and takes a genuine interest in others
- ✓ Builds trust easily
- ✓ Has the time to devote to this endeavor
- ✓ Works hard and doesn't get discouraged easily
- ✓ Is flexible and open to new ideas

✓ Can be a team player and give others credit

✓ Bilingual (if applicable)

Just as I did earlier, Donna and Ron caution that parents who have the potential to become leaders may not know everything or have all of the preceding traits when you meet them, but they will be willing to learn and be trained. (Maybe it should go without saying, but I'll point out here that all of this should be true of you, too.)

In approaching people and asking them to join us, I found myself mostly talking about the time commitment. Who was willing to make the sacrifice of time away from family? Of time spent stuffing envelopes, making phone calls, sitting in meetings, and going to the Capitol? Among those who said, Yes, call me anytime and I'll be there, we had a diverse group: many single moms, a few single dads, one married dad, and a mix of blacks and whites. They were at all economic levels: some of them affluent, some on welfare, and some in the middle. We were working to benefit areas with the lowest income and the worst schools, but people came from all over the city, from all eight wards of the District. Geography, economics, race, and marital status became irrelevant when these parents banded together to help kids.

Be sure you don't discount anyone because *you* think their lives are already too full—only they can let you know the depth of their commitment. Most of our parent leaders already had plenty going on; it's just that this was too important for them not to give their all.

One of our parent leaders was Catherine, a grandmother raising her grandsons in this tough city. Their mother was deceased, and Catherine was determined to do whatever was necessary to ensure that the boys received the best education possible. Even though we spent incredibly long hours walking the halls of the Congressional Office buildings, she was there day after day, anytime I called and asked her to be

7

there. Even though she was uncomfortable speaking in public, she stepped up whenever the need arose for an interview, a hearing, to speak in a meeting—whatever was needed, she was there. She never complained about the heat, the rain, or the hours. She trusted me and was determined to help make sure that the opportunity to receive a voucher was realized.

Another parent leader, Valerie, was going through terrible personal issues, facing losing her home, looking for employment, and dealing with a troubled teen son, but she was determined that her young daughter would have a chance to get a quality education. Often through tears and despite all kinds of obstacles she told me time and time again that she would do whatever was necessary for us to accomplish our goals.

Barbara, a single mother of two, had just been laid off from her job and was worried about how to find another and how to pay her bills when, in the middle of the campaign, she learned her six-year-old son was deaf. Even though this was devastating, and she was working within a difficult system to get him help, she was beside us fighting for this program *every time we called.* Her children had been the recipients of a private scholarship, so she knew how important this program would be for other low-income families, and she was determined to help get it passed.

Step 3. Remind Them That They Have the Right to Speak Out

School choice advocacy is about creating options for children who would otherwise be stuck in failing public schools. In the introduction to this book, I told the story of my son, William, who no doubt would have wound up in jail or worse if we hadn't been able to move him from a dangerous school environment to one that made it safe for him to excel. His story is one of many that I'll be sharing with you throughout this book. Here's another mother's story, told in her own words.

I am a single parent and, in my life, I have been aware of terrible things in D.C. public schools (DCPS), beginning when I was a student there. When I was in high school, a boy was shot and killed at my school. That was a hint to me that I should be somewhere else, and I dropped out.

I later returned to a charter school and graduated while supporting my two children, Delonte and Destinee, and myself. They attended DCPS, and I was unhappy with the quality of the schools they attended, seeing peeling paint and broken bathroom stalls that appeared to just be a part of life. As a volunteer tutor, I saw a student who had been held back two grades but was still getting all the words wrong on a basic spelling test. That student should have been given remedial help but apparently was not helped.

When one of my children scored well above grade level on a standardized test, I discussed wanting to find another school with my child's teacher. The teacher had told me that my child was unlikely to stay above grade level at her school.

It is not easy to find a good school for your children. Parents should not have to worry about guns and knives in school, and you shouldn't have to fight for your kids to learn. All parents should have a choice, and vouchers help give us a chance to expand our search for the best school possible.

—Sherine, single mother of two children

School choice advocacy is also about helping parents find their voices and reminding them that they have the right to speak out. Parents need to know they can make things happen for their children through government. That's powerful! Every parent I know who has participated in education reform has been incredibly moved by the experience. I remember the first time I attended a hearing and won the vote—what a rush! It's truly remarkable to know that, as private citizens with something to say, we can influence people who affect how we live our daily lives. Parents have told me with tears in their eyes how thrilling it is to stand in front of people you watch on TV, have them listen to your story and your plea for change, and then see them act on what you've said.

You start small, and then work your way up. You begin by helping fledgling leaders tell other parents about the campaign and eventually work up to the lights-camera-action stuff. There are a few keys to powerful presentation that every parent leader (and later, every parent) in your organization needs to master:

✓ Tell a personal story
✓ Be brief and to the point
✓ Know what emotions to share

Although you'll want to educate everyone who participates in your organization about all the issues and facts relevant to your campaign, their most powerful influence will be

> ### The Mission of Any School Choice Grassroots Leader
>
> Although the primary purpose of your organization will be to effect a change at the government level, you must adopt a personal mission, as well: *To help parents help themselves understand that to ensure quality education for their children, they must be involved.*
>
> Often, parents in urban communities feel intimidated by schoolteachers, principals, and administrators and are unaware of their own rights and options. It's your job to help them rediscover their influence and express their opinions in ways that will make a difference.

felt when they stand up and deliver their own personal stories. These stories illustrate the power of school choice, both in terms of what it can do for people and what happens when it's absent. Heartfelt stories reach people in ways that facts and figures cannot. Through their personal experience, parents can become influential spokespeople to other parents, community leaders, the media, and the legislature. It's especially important that parent leaders learn to do this, because they are role models for the entire organization.

To engage other people, parents must be brief and to the point. In training volunteers for D.C. Parents for School Choice, we first helped them to write about their experience in just four paragraphs. (You just read an example in Sherine's story.) It's tempting to include every nuance and detail, as everything that has happened to a child can be emotionally charged for a parent. Yet, to be effective, parents need to step back and see the big picture. What were the most significant events? What was the effect on the child? What was the end result? Did the problem get solved? How will/did school choice make the difference?

In this book, you can find several examples of how I've related my own story. On the first page of the introduction, you can read how I told it in two paragraphs when testifying in the Committee on Education in the Workforce hearings. Right after that, you can read an expanded version. And just a few minutes ago, you read that story boiled down into one sentence.

The point is that you and your parent leaders need to be able to say as little or as much as will hold people's attention. Generally, that's about four paragraphs long when you're speaking in front of a group. The last thing you want is for people to start tuning you out because you've gone on too long. Far better to leave them wanting more.

Parents' strong feelings about this issue are an important component of these stories. It's wonderful to see someone beam with pride about the success of a student who has gotten out of a bad situation. It's equally moving to hear parents speak candidly about the pain of how a school or system failed to serve their children. These emotions inspire others to take action. (Later, I'll address in some detail which emotions should *not* be conveyed when you are trying to persuade.)

The goal in sharing any personal story is to connect with people. Then, ideally, you follow up with what advertisers refer to as a "call to action," which means you want to get people excited and raring to go. This can come in the form of delivering brief information about your mission, who your efforts will affect, and how the person listening can help. These final words should be driven largely by the campaign messages you and the parent leaders will map out together, which you'll be guided to construct in chapter 2, "Get the Word Out."

Step 4. Stay in Regular Contact and Let Them Know They Are Vital to the Campaign

Every Thursday or Friday, I met with our parent leader group over lunch. We talked about what we had done, where we were going, and what we had yet to do. We sorted out details and made assignments, but this meal together also let them know that I cared about them, wanted to hear their opinions and ideas, and believed it was crucial to include them in discussions about our plans.

Many of the parents were from low-income families, people who had never been in the public eye before this campaign, parents who until this point had probably never thought that their voices could matter. Nurturing them and my relationship with them was always key.

This luncheon was just one of the outward signs of how much I appreciated them. I'm the first to admit that I often behaved like their mama, hugging them and praising them and beaming all over when they did something wonderful. You will find your own way. You must. The success or failure of your efforts lies entirely with these powerfully motivated, committed, compassionate people.

Parent Leader Training

The job of parent leaders is to help organize activities and to expand the parent base. Ultimately, they will be doing exactly what you did to find them: becoming visible in the community, identifying people who are like-minded and could contribute their time to the campaign, and then helping those people learn to speak out in support of the cause. Parent leaders need to be powerful spokespeople, able to answer both questions and criticism, and prepared for the roller-coaster emotional ride that you will all share together.

To fully coach you in coaching them would require another book, an entire training manual. Fortunately, several good guides have been written on this subject, and they are listed in appendix A, "Recommended Resources." Expect to dedicate at least a couple of weekends to this leadership training, and be sure to schedule the meetings for no more than two hours. The best time is after parents take children to school or before they have to pick them up from school during the week. Be sure to have child care available whenever your meeting is during a time that children have to be with parents.

Think of the people at your meetings as your guests and treat them as if you had invited them into your home. Serve food: meals for lunch meetings and snacks for all meetings. Start and end on time.

Probably the most important thing you can do is listen to what parents have to say about their own issues and lives. Maybe you or your organization can help, or maybe the listening itself is a help. Sometimes people just need to talk.

You'll need to be flexible in your agenda, but any excellent leadership training program will include the following components:

- ✓ Set the expectations for how much time and effort volunteers will need to expend.
- ✓ Inspire everyone with stories of education reform that has been sparked by parent grassroots organizations.
- ✓ Educate them about the history of school choice and debunk the myths surrounding it.

✓ Teach them about the state's legislative process.

✓ Develop specific skills, including such things as running meetings and working together to apply strategies and tactics.

✓ Help them understand the political arena, with its combative atmosphere and shifting interests.

Reading this book will assist you in implementing whatever training program you decide to undertake. It will help you to be an effective leader, guide you in formulating strategies, prepare you for what's ahead, and give you the inside story on what works and what doesn't. We begin the next chapter by helping you go even deeper into the community to gain greater insight into the needs of the parents, as well as to gather those people who will become your all-important volunteer base.

2

Take It to the Streets:
Gathering Support in Your Community

"It is easy to say that parents should speak out, but too often they are silenced by fear or shame: fear of the education establishment and shame of the label placed upon their child and family by this same education establishment. However, the greatest silencer of parents is solitude."
—*Teresa Treat, program director of the CEO Foundation in San Antonio, Texas, from the handbook,* Building the Base: A Blueprint for Grassroots Leaders in the School Choice Movement *by Donna Watson*

Y ou've been there or you've heard the stories. School officials, administrators, and teachers can feel threatened and even become hostile when confronted with the failure to reach a certain child. The kids themselves can seem impossible. It's common indeed for parents to give up because it all seems so hopeless. Many feel as if they're the only ones dealing with the problem, as if they're all alone.

As you know, they're not. Depending on how large a geographic area you hope to serve and the severity of its public school problems, there are probably hundreds or thousands of people in this situation right now, who have no idea that others are going through exactly the same thing. It should be your mission to find them and introduce them to your group so they can see this for themselves. Then these parents can be encouraged not to give up, and their frustration with the system can be galvanized into positive action.

Reaching Out to the Community

In the first chapter, I stressed the importance of making yourself visible so you can meet and recruit people who have the potential to become parent leaders. Once you have this core group established, you are poised to extend your reach to additional parents who are interested in your cause and can form the powerful base of your organization. These people will help you illustrate to the powers-that-be just how widely the issue reaches. They'll be your foot soldiers, the critical mass of people who care about school choice and are willing to stand up and be counted.

How do you find them? With D.C. Parents for School Choice, we got involved with existing parent groups in the area by (1) meeting with adult members of organizations such as neighborhood watches and Boys and Girls Clubs and (2) meeting with parents in alternative schools (private and charter). These are wonderful places to get to know people, to hear their concerns, and to let them know you are their advocate. They also provide access to a large number of parents and enable you to give information that will empower them to make choices for their children.

We also co-sponsored the D.C. Charter School Parent Fair with the Friends of Choice in Urban Schools (FOCUS). More than five hundred parents attended to see representatives from the forty D.C. Public Charter Schools, and this was a terrific opportunity for us, again, to meet people, hear more about their dreams for their children, and provide needed information so they could make good choices.

In the beginning, it was also critical for us to have a table at the local fairs and other gatherings. I attended as many of these events as possible, listening to parents, talking to them about options for their children, letting them know when we'd be getting together next.

Later on, we held large community dinners to celebrate school choice, underwritten by some key financial backers (more on that in chapter 4, "Understand Money Matters"). We occasionally had social gatherings, such as pizza and bowling parties. Though they were restricted to the times when we had the funds to do them, they were an important part of our work because they provided a different setting, a more casual atmosphere than even the friendliest meeting could have. People were comfortable and candid, and we got a different kind of input because of it.

One thing we tried, without much success, was talking with clergy to see if they would help us contact parents in their congregations. I don't think you should let our poor results in this area discourage you from trying this, however. To understate, D.C. is a highly political town. Some of the larger churches participate avidly and, as you know, our issue can be something of a hot potato. This may not be such an obstacle where you live, and you may find some of your greatest advocates among men and women of the cloth.

Perhaps the most significant efforts we made came from providing "Positive Parenting Training Sessions." Aimed at teaching parents how to become more involved in their children's education, these sessions included such topics as "How to Pick a Charter School" and "How to Interact with Administrators and Teachers." As we became more familiar with the issues that were important to parents, we also offered community classes in subjects they said they wanted, such as "Where to Get Free Immunization," "How to Read Your Child's Stanford 9 Scores" (our standardized test in the District), "How 'No Child Left Behind' May Affect Your Family," and "How to Find Great Summer Programs for Your Kids."

During the most active year of our campaign, we held more than one hundred parent meetings. Our objective in these hour-and-a-half (at most) sessions was always to help people better understand the educational system and to know what resources were already in place for providing their kids the best possible learning environments. In D.C., it's common for some of the greatest opportunities to remain hidden from low-income parents, simply because they're on the other side of town. Some programs don't have the funds to promote themselves, so we were a much-needed clearinghouse of information about our community.

For example, the University of D.C. offers one of my favorites, a program that's been operating for about twenty years. If a child has an interest in and an aptitude for science or math, he or she can attend UDC free for a whole summer, and it can also lead to college scholarships. I knew about the program because my oldest son, Michael, had been an academic standout, had a teacher who was on the ball, and eventually earned one of their scholarships. When I asked if we might help them promote the program in low-income areas, they were delighted. If we had not been there, spreading the word, people in the communities we served would never have heard about it.

My daughter, Miashia, also participated in a little-known program, one for minority student journalists held at Howard University and hosted by Time Warner Inc. I found out about it from a *Washington Post* reporter who had written an article on high school newspapers and clued me in. The program had been in existence for years, yet a D.C. student had never participated until my daughter did.

These are only two of many hidden treasures we unearthed, including a research program at the National Institutes of Health, some programs that offered a stipend for participants, and some that were just for fun.

What programs may be undiscovered in your own community? I highly recommend that you do something similar for the parents near you so they can find out what's available to them right now for getting their kids more excited about learning and life.

Let People Know Where You'll Be

To invite parents to a meeting, whether we were hosting it ourselves or participating as part of someone else's schedule, we sent flyers to a mailing list. We developed the list by gathering names and contact information everywhere we went, using a simple card that concerned parents could fill out and return to us. We entered the information into a database so we could stay in touch and easily organize parents into workgroups. If I needed twenty-five parents to go to Capitol Hill with me, for example, parent leaders could access the database, collect all the names and phone numbers of those who said they wanted to demonstrate with me, and then call to see who would be available.

But we didn't rely only on the database. Our neighborhoods had enough people moving in and out that, to reach new folks, we walked our notices all over town. Our twenty-seven local libraries posted them for us (fortunately, there was a central distribution point so that we simply had to go there to get them out everywhere). We put them in self-service laundries, Boys and Girls Clubs, and community centers. We also developed a relationship with fourteen of the public housing managers, who agreed to put them into mailboxes or hang them in central areas.

What's more, we loved to call radio shows and try to get on the air so we could tell about our upcoming event. (See the next chapter for specific tips on how to handle yourself on-air.)

Finally, my refrain to parent leaders was never to go anywhere without flyers to give people. This way, when you're talking with someone, it's easy to say, "Come to this event if you can. If you can't, just give us a call so we can talk some more about your choices." I always had flyers and volunteer cards in the trunk of my car, and I carried a simple business card with our organization's phone number.

Sample Volunteer Card (Front Side)

My child's education is my first priority.

❑ Sign me up! I want to volunteer to help D.C. kids get a better education!

(Check all that apply.)

❑ I believe some children have needs that would best be served by a different school (public or private).

❑ I believe politicians need to hear from real mothers and fathers.

❑ I am willing to pass out flyers.

❑ I am willing to tell my story to members of Congress.

❑ I am willing to get parents at my child's school to sign a petition for scholarships.

❑ I will attend meetings to show my support.

❑ I am willing to call 10 friends to ask them to support scholarships.

❑ I will help with events for scholarships.

Name _____

Address _____

City _____ State _____ ZIP _____ E-mail _____

Phone (h) _____ (w) _____ (c) _____

Best way to reach: ❑ E-mail   ❑ Phone   ❑ Mail

(Circle all that apply.)

My children attend:
   Public School, Private School, Charter School, Home School

My children are ages: _____

Sample Volunteer Card (Back Side)

My friends are interested in a better education for their kids.

Please send information on how they can help, too:

#1 Name _____

Address _____

City _____ State _____ ZIP _____

Phone: _____ E-mail _____

#2 Name _____

Address _____

City _____ State _____ ZIP _____

Phone: _____ E-mail _____

It's hard to say how our statistics might translate to your situation, but here's some food for thought. Before each event, we'd run off a thousand copies of our flyers on the cheapest paper we could find. At each meeting, we could expect to see between fifty and seventy-five people, including both parents and their children. Typically, about half were new and the other half were people who were devoted, making it to every meeting and often bringing along friends and family members. About a third of the new people would indicate they wanted to help when they filled out our volunteer cards. This means that, for every meeting we held, we were continuing our service to more than twenty-five people, meeting up to forty more, and bringing somewhere between eight and twenty new ones into the campaign.

Sample Flyer #1

DC PARENTS FOR SCHOOL CHOICE

Date: 06/15/03
Time: 10AM-1:00 PM

Give parents a choice, give children a chance!

Educating our children in Washington, DC

SCHOOL CHOICE FOR DC CHILDREN
PARENT VOICES MAKE A DIFFERENCE!

Come and join us on the Hill. Let's let the politicians know that DC Parents do want choices for their children. DC Public Schools are in need of serious reform. Our children need options now. We can't wait years for reform. No child should be lost to the system. Show your support by going to the Hill and letting your voice be heard.

Highlights

♦ Transportation provided

♦ Lunch Provided

♦ Wear your DC Parents for School Choice T-shirt (one will be provided for those who don't have one)

♦ Children are welcome

When: June 15, 2003
Where: 3rd & Independence Ave., SE
Time: 10 AM to 1 PM

Pick Up:

SE Locations:
Trenton Terrace at 9:15 AM
Safeway at Alabama Ave., SE at 9:30 AM

NW Locations
Hamilton Rec Center 9:15 AM
North Capitol and K St., 9:30 AM

Or meet at us the Rayburn Building at 10 AM:
3rd & Independence Ave., SW
Take blue line to Capitol South Metro Stop

DC PARENTS FOR SCHOOL CHOICE

809 Virginia Avenue, SE
WDC 20003

Phone: 202 546 4304
Fax: 202 546 4305
Email: wdcparentschoice@aol.com

Sample Flyer #2

 DC PARENTS FOR SCHOOL CHOICE Date: 05/09/03
Time: 6:30-8:00 PM

Give parents a choice, give children a chance!
Educating our children in Washington, DC

LET'S TALK ABOUT THE STANFORD NINE.

Come and join us. Let's talk about how to read the Stanford Nine Test. Parents receive these all important test scores that are so critical to the schools. How do parents interpret these tests. What do the classifications mean and what impact do they have for our children. Learn what the test means and how to talk to your child's teacher about the results.

Highlights

♦ Parents need options for their children who are in low performing schools. Learn how you can make a difference! Join *DC Parents for School Choice* by going to Capitol Hill to show your support of Vouchers for DC children.

When: May 9, 2003
Where: Lamond Riggs Library
Time: 6:30-8:00 PM

Lamond Riggs is located at :
5401 South Dakota Ave., NE
Phone: 202 541-6255

 DC PARENTS FOR SCHOOL CHOICE

809 Virginia Avenue, SE
WDC 20003

Phone: 202 546 4304
Fax: 202 546 4305
Email: wdcparentschoice@aol.com

Sample Flyer #3

**DC PARENTS FOR
SCHOOL CHOICE**

**Date: 02/25/03
Time: 6:30-7:30 PM**

Give parents a choice, give children a chance!
Educating our children in Washington, DC

LET'S TALK ABOUT EDUCATION IN D.C.

Come and join us. Let's talk about the education
issues that are currently before us. There are
many worrisome issues that need to be addressed
immediately. What can we do? How can we help?
How can we keep our children safe? What are our
options? D. C. Parents for School Choice seeks to
unite parents voices to effect positive changes in
Washington, D.C.

Highlights
♦ There will be a Town Hall meeting at
GMCHC Family Life Community Center,
605 Rhode Island Ave., N.E. regarding
proposed Child Welfare Laws on
February 26, 2003 from 6 to 8:30PM

When: February 25, 2003
Where: Francis A. Gregory Library
Time: 6:30-7:30 PM

Francis A. Gregory Library is located at :
Alabama Avenue and 37th St., SE.
Phone: 202 645 4297

**DC PARENTS FOR
SCHOOL CHOICE**

809 Virginia Avenue
WDC 20003

Phone: 202 546 4304
Fax: 202 546 4305
Email: wdcparentschoice@aol.com

Conduct the Meetings Yourself

Yes, you read that right. I believe the leader of the organization should attend every meeting and not delegate hosting responsibilities. You should be the one to welcome guests, introduce any speakers, and keep the group moving forward according to its agenda. This isn't because I believe in power tripping—hardly! Believe me, it would be much easier to just let someone else take over some of the time. But it's crucial for you to build personal credibility by consistently showing how much you care about every single issue your grassroots group will address.

My twin sister, Harrietta, teases me about being five hundred people's best friend. She says everyone acts like they know me personally, and in a way that's because they do. Anyone who's attended one of our meetings knows one of the single most important things about me: I am a tireless advocate for this cause. Actually, it's not truthful to say I don't get tired. It's more accurate to say I don't let that get in the way of my commitments.

As the leader, you must become the most recognizable member of your organization. Everybody knows there were hundreds of people who led the civil rights effort. But who do people remember? Dr. Martin Luther King—not because he's the only one who made a difference, but because he was there, as the key spokesperson and leader, making a point and a clear case whenever people would listen. Likewise, in our cause, there are many wonderful people involved, but there must be one face the people will remember, the primary leader.

In time, you'll be shopping in the supermarket and have people stop to tell you they know you from somewhere. That's because you and your parent leaders will have made sure that your campaign is reaching people *everywhere.*

Be Part of a Community Coalition

In our campaign, I was incredibly lucky to have been part of a local coalition of community and business leaders who were committed to persuading legislators that school choice was a reasonable, desirable solution for District parents and students. Calling ourselves the "D.C. Coalition," we were an informal group of the movers and shakers who cared most about opportunity scholarships. The group included a representative from the Archdiocese of Washington (most placements in D.C. are with Catholic schools because 50 percent of the private schools here are parochial), representatives from independent private schools, staffers from the mayor's office, businesspeople and others who provide private scholarships, and leaders from a couple of other organizations that support kids in the District.

We met to strategize and to update one another on all that was happening in our particular areas of focus. My job was strictly to garner the voices and faces of the parents who would be most affected by school choice legislation. The idea, of course, was that the more people who would come out, the better we could demonstrate community support, and the greater our influence would be on the Hill.

The role of D.C. Parents for School Choice was always crystal clear among members of the coalition. More than once, they said to me, "As long as you're out there, doing your bit, then we know we can move forward. We're confident that when we say, 'The people of D.C. want this,' we're telling the truth. You're backing us up, which is the most important thing you can do."

Some members of the coalition lobbied directly. Others focused on talking to the private schools to make sure there was sufficient space for scholarship students. Still others worked with legislators and local politicians to help draft the proposed legislation.

Nobody really formed the D.C. Coalition; it just grew organically out of our shared commitment. As our parent group gathered steam and started getting noticed by the media, people began contacting me. You can do it the same way I did, which was strictly to focus on the parents and let the rest take care of itself, or you can seek out other supporters right from the start and suggest that you begin meeting regularly so you can work together in your campaign. Either way, I suggest you don't try to take on the role of being head of a coalition, too. The single most important thing you can contribute as a grassroots leader is to stay attuned to the people you hope to serve: listening to their needs, helping them connect with one another, and offering them resources they can use right now.

Before we move on to the next chapter and the head-spinning topic of media, to help you implement what you've been reading thus far, I'm including a checklist you can use in getting your group off the ground. These first two steps—recruiting parent leaders and reaching out to the parents in the community—are the key to your campaign.

If this list makes it look like a lot of work, that's only because it is. I figure it's not my job to take advantage of your enthusiasm by puffing you up with false expectations. Instead, my goal is to give you a sense of what it really takes and to assure you that *it can be done.* We did it here in D.C., and we were not the first. You're an extraordinary person just because you're considering taking this on. If you decide you're up to the challenge, I wish you great resources of time and energy, as well as wonderful parents who care deeply about school choice. You're about to embark on one of the most rewarding and challenging endeavors of your life!

Checklist for Recruiting Parent Leaders and Reaching Parents

Become visible and knowledgeable about the parents around you:

❑ Volunteer to help with community projects.

❑ Tell people about your commitment to school choice.

❑ Share your personal story.

❑ Get to know the neighborhood heroes.

Identify people who will be good advocates and invite them to become parent leaders:

❑ Consider everyone you meet.

❑ Consult your neighborhood heroes.

❑ Let them know there will be a serious time commitment.

Remind parents that they have the right to speak out:

❑ Help them find their own voices.

❑ Help them learn to tell their unique stories briefly and with passion.

Support your parent leaders:

❑ Stay in regular contact and let them know they are vital to the campaign.

❑ Have weekly lunch meetings.

❑ Give regular and sincere praise for their hard work.

❑ Train them (refer to appendix A, "Recommended Resources," for ideas and help).

Use existing organizations to help you meet parents:

❏ Meet with adult members of neighborhood and community organizations.

❏ Meet with parents in alternative schools.

Be visible in community events:

❏ Participate in or sponsor educational fairs.

❏ Have a table at any local gatherings.

Host events where parents can meet one another and learn together:

❏ Ask parents what issues concern them most—then offer training and resources in those areas.

❏ Hold social events that will allow parents to feel more relaxed than they would in formal meetings.

❏ Be a clearinghouse for information parents need to get their kids excited about learning and life.

Get the word out to as many parents as possible:

❏ Gather names and contact information wherever you go.

❏ Develop a database and send information to your mailing list.

❏ Post flyers in as many places as possible (libraries, laundries, community centers, etc.).

❏ Call in to radio shows and talk about the upcoming event.

❏ Never go anywhere without flyers and volunteer cards.

❏ Attend and lead every single meeting your group hosts.

Be part of a community coalition:

❑ Either participate in or initiate a coordinated effort in your area.

❑ Stay focused on your role: listening to parents' needs, helping them to connect with one another, offering them resources they can use right now, gathering them together to demonstrate how powerfully committed you all are.

3

Get the Word Out:
Working with the Media

"The African-American moms who turned out to demonstrate for school choice . . . did so even though they knew they would be largely ignored by the mainstream media. The scales now falling from the eyes of local Democratic leaders attest to the unflagging persistence of these ordinary moms and dads.

"In short, the alliance for school choice has helped bring public pressure to bear on what is in essence a civil rights proposition: that the mostly African-American kids now condemned to rot in failing D.C. public schools deserve a real shot at a decent education. They have persevered, and it looks as though they shall soon overcome."

From the editorial pages of the Wall Street Journal, *May 11, 2003*

In every press release, rally, interview, public service announcement, flyer, newsletter article, bus placard, and T-shirt, our message was always the same: "Parents deserve a choice so their kids can have a chance."

This wasn't because we couldn't think of anything else to say. On the contrary, our biggest challenge was to *keep everyone focused* on this message and to help them not get so caught up in what was happening that they'd say the wrong thing, or say too much. If there's one, single most important piece of advice I can give you about the media, it's that you'd better be clear about what you want to say, and then stick to it.

You simply must resist the temptation to confide in, over-explain, or otherwise attempt to persuade representatives of the media by talking too much. It seems harmless to give people the "inside story" when you think they are sympathetic to your cause, but you need to understand something a couple of reporters taught me early on: "We may like you, Virginia, and we may even think you are in the right, but our job is to find the story. So don't tell us anything you don't want to see in print."

Then what can you tell the media? Whatever you and your group have decided in advance is appropriate. You must plan what you'll say to people outside your organization, support those assertions with carefully checked facts, and then *follow the plan.*

Your job, as the leader of a grassroots organization, is to help everyone else understand this, too. Various media outlets can be powerful boons to your campaign, including everything from TV coverage of your rallies and presence at hearings to the brief blurb in the community paper about when parents will be getting together next. But beware: The media is not unlike a wild animal. Handle it with care, keep your cool, and know how it behaves, and you might walk away with only a few scratches and get bitten just a few times. But get too close, treat it poorly, or forget what you're really dealing with, and you'll probably get mauled.

This may sound overly dramatic, but it's not. I can tell you that our contact with the media was both gratifying and intensely frustrating, and despite careful strategizing, we sometimes stepped in it. We even had a few run-ins that I considered dangerous. You'll learn what steps we took in this chapter: I'll give you the truth about what worked, what didn't, and what blew up in our faces. I'll even tell you about the few things that were inexplicably difficult, that couldn't be foreseen or controlled once they were underway—and what we did about them.

Understand Your Role

The first step is to get clear on the role of the parent group in the larger scheme of things. While legislators debate the merits, and backers put their money up to help further the campaign, *the moms and dads put a real face on the issue for the public.* Stay focused on this role, and your interactions with the media can be positive for the most part.

In establishing a core media message, seek guidance. I talked to everyone I knew and trusted, asking, "What do you think? How should we present this?"

We were incredibly fortunate to have the assistance of a libertarian public interest law firm, the Institute for Justice. They put their public relations and legal resources at our disposal, and both were crucial. Whenever we needed advice about how to handle a delicate issue, they were indispensable. When we wanted to release information to the media, they helped us do so in the most effective way possible. They were also a key referral source whenever we needed to find professional help for some other aspect of the campaign.

I also consulted my reporter friends, one who works at the *Washington Times* and the other who works at the *Washington Post* (neither are on the education beat), to learn about what the media would "buy." For those of us who are not journalists, it can be difficult to see what will or won't get media attention. It's easy to be caught up in our own ideas about what's interesting or what other people should be interested in. For example, don't statistics on dropout rates and violence in schools get your goat? Doesn't it make you crazy when you realize how long it's taking to get a solution for public school students? Wouldn't you think this would make a news story?

We found that the media was most interested in us not when we were spouting facts or crying out for a solution; instead, they paid attention when we just *showed up.* Journalists thought it was newsworthy when our group of parents marched to demand better choices for the District's children, when our passion for this issue was evident in our actions, when we started telling stories about our own kids and the kids we knew.

The first time we ever got any coverage was at a city council meeting where one hundred parents arrived and twenty testified in support of vouchers. The buzz was that there was this incredible amount of interest, so we went with it. We let the media know anytime we were going to gather in large numbers. My first interviews all sounded like this: "We have an incredibly strong base, and our parents are committed." In truth, there were times when technically we had ten people in the organization, but the community was always behind us, so it was just a matter of finding a strong way to position it. We wouldn't inflate our numbers for the press, but we didn't disabuse them of the notion that we had lots of people on board, either.

This goes back to not saying too much. Don't tell the media more than they need to know, because then they'll have all kinds of choices about how to position you. Instead, you set the tone by sticking to a media message you all have agreed is the right one to move the campaign forward.

In time, as the media became more familiar with us, they did contact us to talk about the issues and not just to find out how many parents belonged to our organization. Eventually, they trusted us enough that they sought me out when they wanted to verify facts for their stories. Although it wasn't technically a "strategy"—it was something we did just because it was right—it bears mentioning that absolute accuracy in any information you share is imperative. Start shading the truth or making mistakes, and you're bound to get caught—and worse, destroy your credibility. On the other hand, be completely sure of your facts, and you will become a trusted source.

Most of my contact with the media was cordial and constructive. One reporter would cover just about anything we were doing, so whenever we had an event, I gave her a call.

Know that you can and will form that kind of relationship with the media if you are consistently a source of good information. If your efforts are regularly profiled, it builds wonderful credibility in the community and augments whatever other methods you are using to communicate with the parents. It has gotten to the point now that, wherever I go, people will say, "Gee, I know you from somewhere." That's simply because we made it our business to get our cause featured, our faces seen, and our voices heard everywhere we could.

Not every story written about you will be flattering or even accurate. There were times I was misquoted or completely taken out of context. We were roundly criticized by some groups, and I was personally attacked in print on more than one occasion. I was insulted often. Being called "phony," a "sellout," and a "mouthpiece" were probably the most hurtful, and I regularly cried over what I read.

On one occasion, a reporter went way, way too far. She was writing for the *Common Denominator,* a small paper distributed in my family's neighborhood. She called to interview me and was incredibly insistent and rude in her questioning. Honestly, I've been interviewed hundreds of times, and this was a first. I told her that if she couldn't be civil with me, I would not finish the conversation, which made her angry. I wound up terminating the interview before we'd really finished. Her article appeared in the paper with horrible, accusatory inaccuracies. I called to give her the correct information, which was not a particularly pleasant conversation, either. At some point she called the IRS, assuming that D.C. Parents for School choice was a 501(c)(3) nonprofit organization and that we could be caught in some irregularity. (It wasn't and we weren't.) The capper was when the paper published a picture of my house and listed my address to accompany more of her bile. As a result, I received my first death threat.

How did I respond? At home, I was a wreck, worried that my family was in danger. I called the police, who sent patrol cars for about a week, and although my husband and I considered hiring private security, we decided not to do so. But I made no public response. This was our strategy anytime we were attacked, either personally or as a group: No returning volley, no crying foul. In time, the fervor died down, and in the end, the paper and its rogue reporter did catch some heat for their actions, as even the *Wall Street Journal* ran a piece condemning such a total disregard for my privacy and safety.

As the leader, you must set an example and be impeccable in your dealings with the media. My personal experience is that, in most cases, measured, calm responses endear you to reporters over the long run. While a screaming fit may make a headline, it won't invite people to come back to you with any consistency or to find you particularly believable. Instead, strive to be the voice of reason, compassion, and deeply held conviction. As you've heard hundreds of times before, you catch more flies with honey than with vinegar.

Should You Ever "Go Negative"?

The short answer to the question of whether there's ever a time to use negativity in your campaign is yes. Sometimes it's needed. Sometimes you have to be clear about your opposition and why you believe they're wrong.

We started out trying to be the nice guys in the voucher movement, attempting to advocate using only positive comments and actions. At the risk of sounding immodest, I have to tell you that this was primarily because I am a nice person, and the parents I had around me were all lovely people.

No matter how nice you are, however, the media will look for an angle. They will look for the negative, so you have to be vigilant if you want to maintain a positive position. One reporter actually told me straight out, "Come on, Virginia. Give me the dirt."

My response: "I don't know any dirt. I'm only going to tell you what we're doing." End of story.

Although, as I said, there is a time and place for negativity, clearly, circumstances like that don't qualify. I still feel strongly that you must be choosy. I've never been in favor of attacking the public schools, for example, partly because my parents were public school educators and I know how much they cared and how hard they worked for their students, and partly because it's counterproductive. I just don't think it's a constructive tactic. Instead, we looked for ways to benefit the public schools, too, and ultimately, we were able to pass a bill that not only included vouchers but also provided increased funding for the public and charter schools in D.C. We always stated our position this way:

**"We are working toward improvement
in the public school system. In the meanwhile,
parents need a choice . . ."**

Yet there were times when the kid gloves came off. For example, there were points in the campaign where we felt compelled to publicly criticize members of Congress. In particular, Senator Mary Landrieu (D-La.) shocked us by reversing her position on school choice in 2003 during an Appropriations Committee hearing. Landrieu, who had led us to believe she would vote yea, stood up and gave a damning presentation to the Senate, then voted nay.

To make matters worse, dismayed parents were gathered in the corridor afterward when nine-year-old Mosiyah Hall asked Landrieu where she sent her own children to school. She told him they attended Georgetown Day, a private school in D.C. She then turned to the assembled parents and remarked that vouchers wouldn't help them, because Georgetown Day was too expensive and they still wouldn't be able to afford it. Incredible! She had no idea what the income levels of the parents were, or really anything at all about the hopes of the people who were standing gape-mouthed in front of her.

It was clear to us that Landrieu just didn't get it. We decided to call her on her condescension and point out the unfairness of letting income dictate whether parents had a choice about what school their children would attend. Our objective was to send a message to all the members of Congress that their position was not going unnoticed, and that there would be consequences for disingenuous posturing. With funding from a key financial backer, we decided to launch an advertising campaign with newspaper ads appearing in the New Orleans *Times-Picayune*, the most widely read paper in Landrieu's home state.

As you can see on the next page, this was not a "nice" ad. Was it factual? Of course. Was it effective? You bet.

We wound up doing something similar a few months later after Senator Edward Kennedy (D-Mass.) promised to filibuster to obstruct our school voucher bill. This came right on the heels of Senator Dianne Feinstein (D-Calif.) making her own switch, this one in our favor, thus setting up what the *Wall Street Journal* called a "bloody battle on the Senate floor." In short, I appeared in a TV spot asking Senator Kennedy how he could turn his back on Bobby and Jack Kennedy's civil-rights legacy and deny children a shot at a decent education. As a huge fan of JFK and his brother, I was loath to criticize anyone in the family. But this was a time when something needed to be said—and the media helped us get the message across loud and clear.

Once you get engaged in the political process, you have to play the game of managing your image, setting the tone, and influencing other people's perceptions. My counsel is that you don't play the media's game. Don't talk "off the record." Don't deliver the dirt. Don't go negative for no reason. This is a rough-and-tumble sport, and it's not always apparent what you need to do to win. Instead, focus, focus, and focus some more on your own objective: putting a real face on the issue for the public so

My mom wanted you to know that

Senator Mary Landrieu

doesn't want me to go to the same school where her children go!

Mosiyah Hall
Washington, D.C.

FACTS

- D.C. public schools are ranked among the very worst in the entire nation.
- Per pupil spending in D.C. is among the very highest in the nation (almost double the per pupil spending in New Orleans).
- Thousands of single Black mothers in D.C. have applied for money so they can transfer their children into a good private or religious school, where they will have a real chance to learn.
- A proposal before Congress would let them do that.
- This proposal has been endorsed by the elected Mayor of D.C. and the president of the D.C. Public School Board.
- Senator Landrieu recently told a group of single Black moms "NO!"-- she will not support this proposal. Then, 9-year old Mosiyah Hall (pictured above) asked the Senator where she sends her kids to school. An irritated Senator Landrieu replied "Georgetown Day," an expensive, <u>private</u> school in D.C.

THAT'S WHY WE BELIEVE

- Public Teacher Unions oppose legislation that would require them to send their own children to public schools, but they support legislation forcing us to do so.
- Politicians like Mary Landrieu apparently care more about what the union wants than they do about poor kids and what their moms want.

Forty years ago, politicians stood in the doors of good schools trying to prevent poor students from getting in.

- That was wrong and Congress changed it.

Today they are standing in the doors of bad schools refusing to let poor students out.

- It's still wrong and Congress and Senator Landrieu should change it.

Alicia Hall-Vicks
Washington, D.C.

"My name is Alicia Hall-Vicks, and I was one of the moms who asked Senator Landrieu for help in making sure my child gets a good education. She told me, 'NO,' and it was my son who asked her where she sends her children to school in D.C.

"So you can understand how mad I got, when I later found out that Black folk in Louisiana gave 95% of their votes to her in the last election, because based on how she treats Black folk here in D.C., she doesn't deserve that kind of support."

"IF D.C. PUBLIC SCHOOLS AREN'T GOOD ENOUGH FOR SENATOR LANDRIEU'S CHILDREN, WHY DOES SHE BELIEVE THEY'RE GOOD ENOUGH FOR MY CHILD?"

Paid for by D.C. Parents for School Choice

that, in the end, legislation gets passed that makes a difference for the children.

Use All Aspects of the Media

Those ads were expensive; I won't kid you about that. Does this mean you have to enjoy a big budget to get the word out? Absolutely not. We started out on a shoestring, and we still keep most expenses to a minimum. In addition to paid advertising in print and on TV, following are various ways we presented ourselves to the media, most of which cost nothing or close to it:

- ✓ Sending news releases to local media (radio, television, and print)
- ✓ Providing public service announcements (PSAs) on radio and television
- ✓ Posting information on community bulletin boards
- ✓ Participating in radio call-in shows
- ✓ Appearing on public television
- ✓ Giving information to neighborhood or community organization newsletters
- ✓ Distributing flyers
- ✓ Writing letters to the editor
- ✓ Wearing our signature T-shirts every time we appeared somewhere together

Although you don't have to be an expert to do any of this yourself, you'll definitely benefit from some expert advice. For example, writing news releases (also called "press releases") and PSAs takes a bit of finesse, and they need to follow a format. Media professionals won't even read them if they don't, so learn this to be sure your work doesn't wind up in the recycling bin. Samples of a news release and a PSA we used during our campaign appear on the next couple of pages.

Sample News Release

D.C. Parents for School Choice

809 Virginia Avenue, SE, Washington D.C. 20011
(202) 546-4304

D.C. Parents for School Choice Celebrates House of Representatives Victory for Parental Choice

FOR IMMEDIATE RELEASE
December 8, 2003

CONTACT:
Virginia Walden Ford
(202) 546-4304

Washington, D.C.—The U.S. House of Representatives approved historic legislation giving low-income children in the District of Columbia the freedom to select private schools through parental choice scholarships. D.C. Parents for School Choice, which represents hundreds of D.C. parents, praised the action:

"Our struggle is nearing an end, as low-income D.C. families are one step away from liberation from failing schools," said Virginia Walden Ford, executive director of D.C. Parents for School Choice, who has been working to secure school choice for the District of Columbia for more than five years.

"We hope the Senate will quickly put the final stamp of approval on D.C. choice by passing the spending package," said Walden Ford. "D.C. parents cannot wait another day for educational freedom."

# # #

Sample Public Service Announcement Script

D.C. Parents for School Choice
809 Virginia Avenue, SE,
Washington D.C. 20011

: 90 SEC. PRE-RECORDED RADIO SPOT

THE HARD TRUTH ABOUT SCHOOLS IN WASHINGTON IS THAT WE HAVE ONE SYSTEM FOR FAMILIES WHO CAN AFFORD TO SEND THEIR CHILDREN TO THE BEST SCHOOLS, AND ANOTHER SYSTEM FOR FOLKS WHOSE CHILDREN ARE TRAPPED IN SCHOOLS THAT ARE NOT WHAT THEY SHOULD BE.

RIGHT NOW, CONGRESS IS CONSIDERING A PROGRAM THAT WOULD INCREASE FUNDING FOR WASHINGTON'S PUBLIC SCHOOLS.

AND IT WOULD GIVE LOW-INCOME FAMILIES SCHOLARSHIP AWARDS, SO WE COULD MAKE THE SAME CHOICES AS HIGH-INCOME FAMILIES.

I'M VIRGINIA WALDEN FORD, EXECUTIVE DIRECTOR OF D.C. PARENTS FOR SCHOOL CHOICE.

WE THINK LOW-INCOME FAMILIES IN WASHINGTON DESERVE THE SAME FREEDOM TO CHOOSE THEIR SCHOOLS.

THAT'S WHY CITIZENS GROUPS THROUGHOUT THE DISTRICT HAVE JOINED TOGETHER TO GAIN PASSAGE OF THE SCHOLARSHIPS BILL.

PLEASE CALL CONGRESS. TELL THEM TO PASS THE D.C. SCHOOLS BILL, AND GIVE US THE KEY TO OPEN THE DOORS TO BETTER SCHOOLS.

#

Just as it makes sense to learn how to write effective news releases and PSAs, you're smart to get some training before you appear on TV or participate in a radio interview. Here's an effective radio strategy I learned from a media expert, for example. While being interviewed briefly about D.C. Parents for School Choice, I would keep the focus on whatever key event was coming up, citing the date and giving our phone number. Then there would usually be a call-in part of the show. The host would speak to a caller, who would usually ask something specific, and I would respond with essentially the same information as I'd provided earlier.

Someone would ask, "How much money do you hope to get for school vouchers?"

As you know, there is no simple answer to that question, so I would always respond, "That is exactly the type of thing we'll be discussing at our meeting on such and such date. You can get more information by calling this phone number."

Next caller: "How can you take money away from the public schools?"

My response: "We are working toward improvement in the public school system. Meanwhile, parents need a choice, and that's what we'll be discussing at our meeting on such and such date. You can get more information by calling this phone number."

And so on. My job was always to mention the information about the upcoming event as many times as possible in the time I had on the air. Try it. You'll get excellent turnout at your meetings!

If you don't have a local advocacy group to give you advice like this and help you the way the Institute for Justice helped us, seek out local public relations firms and ask if they can give you some of their time pro bono. In other words, see if there are professionals in your area who are willing to teach you at no charge about how to interact with the media. Here's a suggestion about how to get the ball rolling:

"We are a parents' organization working to influence legislative decisions about school funding. Is there someone in your office who would be willing to help us by teaching us how to effectively work with the media?"

In addition, if you are working closely with legislative staff members, they can usually help. In particular, a press secretary can be an excellent choice to assist you with media training, both for you and for the parents.

Train Parents to Be Public Speakers

Now, this is a case of don't do as I did, which was to learn by making mistakes, but instead, please do as I say. Just as I suggested that you get media training (I didn't and regretted it), I highly recommend that you train your parents for the media, too.

Initially, we didn't do this, and we had a few loose cannons. One parent would misstate facts. (Even things like how many classes a child has failed can and will be double-checked.) Another would repeat things she'd been told in confidence; I think it was because she got excited and distracted and just plain forgot that she wasn't supposed to divulge those particular things. Yet another loved the spotlight, would descend on any reporter within fifty feet, and then, you guessed it, always said too much. This last woman actually became an asset for us, an articulate and enthusiastic spokesperson—*after* we got her some media training.

Being gracious and well-spoken with the media is a skill anyone can learn. Helping parents to find their voice—to stand up for what they believe and to have that make a difference in the legislative process—is one of the most gratifying parts of leading an organization like this.

All of our parent leaders participated in media training sessions we conducted with the help of a public relations firm who donated their time to us, plus additional assistance from the Institute for Justice. Believe me, it was worth it!

Not too long after, we took about two dozen parents to attend a Congressional hearing. Let me set the scene for you: When you sit in the galley in the Capitol, you're in an immense room with all these people you've seen on TV. You have to sit still and be quiet. No distractions from what is happening on the floor are tolerated. The parents held hands and prayed, and it was an impressive show of solidarity for the two House members who had invited us there: Representatives Tom Davis (R-Va.) and John Boehner (R-Ohio).

Afterward, the Congressmen were the focus of a press conference, but the parents were also asked to attend. We went into the press room and there were, I imagine, representatives from every possible media outlet—radio, television, and print. It was a lovely room filled with people, again, whom we'd all seen on TV.

At some point, the press corps took an interest in the parents. I stepped back and watched in awe. They were incredible! They were so self-assured and articulate about this whole issue, and I remember feeling like a proud mama. As I stood there, I remembered that most of them had not ever spoken in front of a group before, much less the national media. Yet here they were, speaking from their hearts with riveting stories and palpable conviction. It was wonderful!

It's a reasonable goal for everyone in your organization to be able to do this, too. The best part of it is that you don't have to become something you're not: You all get to remain exactly who you are, dedicated to creating new choices for parents and providing better chances for children.

4

Understand Money Matters:
Getting the Financial Backing You Need

"We know what is at stake: the lives and the futures of children, who want to read, learn, study, grow, and live. We want every child to get the most out of his or her educational opportunity, because of the value of an individual's education and then the contributions made by all of our students when they grow and mature. A good, wise, just, and compassionate country makes certain that education opportunities are available for all of its citizens—every single one of them."

From the concluding remarks of former U.S. Secretary of Education Rod Paige at the Office of Innovation and Improvement's Innovations in Education Exchange Series, February 25, 2004

In the early days of D.C. Parents for School Choice, we accomplished a great deal with very little. We squeaked by on pocket change, making every cent go as far as possible. My husband, Earl, likes to say I can stretch a dollar from here to California.

Yet there came a time when we had to seek larger sums of money, and that day will come for you, too. Invoices for copying will mount up. Buying lunches and T-shirts can run into the hundreds of dollars. Just these basics will require that you seek some financial support. Whether you plan to operate on a shoestring (believe me, it can be done and done well), or to use more expensive strategies like advertising, at some point you'll find yourself engaged in fundraising.

If you're like me, asking for money does not come naturally. If it does, more power to you! But for those who find themselves feeling reluctant even to read this chapter, much less actually go out and ask people for help, I hope to simplify this for you and make it a bit more enjoyable. You can think of the process of getting the financial backing you need in four broad strokes:

1. *Decide on the type of legal entity* for your organization with the help of knowledgeable professionals.

2. *Develop your board of directors* to include the active, influential members of your community who care about school choice.

3. *Remember, money is not a four-letter word:* Get out there and ask for it.

4. *Let your conscience be your guide.* Beware of money with strings attached.

This chapter should give you solid footing to go forward and begin your fundraising efforts. It will not, however, deliver all the tools you need to do this on your own. That's because I don't recommend you attempt to bite off this big piece and chew it all by yourself. At a minimum, you'll need to seek out professionals to help you with tax and legal questions, and you'll also benefit from the advice of a professional fundraiser. If you can't afford and don't know any fundraisers who can help you, then you'll need to do some additional study. The Internet is filled with resources for nonprofit organizations, with information on everything from board development to holding fundraising events. Your local bookstore and library should prove a gold mine, too.

Does the success or failure of your campaign hinge on your ability to fundraise? Probably not. However, money does matter. Do your homework, surround yourself with people you trust, and you should be able to finance whatever activities will best serve your parent members and your cause.

Step 1. Decide on the Type of Legal Entity

Before you start accepting anyone's money, you need to determine what kind of organization you want to establish. In other words, what type of legal entity will it be?

It might seem appealing to become a 501(c)(3) nonprofit organization because you would be exempt from taxes under the Internal Revenue Code and, perhaps more important, people could make tax-deductible donations. Yet this kind of organization is also prohibited from lobbying elected officials more than 5 percent of its time, unless it has taken the 501(h) election, which allows it to use up to 20 percent of its resources for lobbying.

We found even 20 percent too restrictive. That's why D.C. Parents for School Choice became a 501(c)(4) organization, which allows us to spend 50 percent of our time and money on advocacy. We devote the other half to the work we do in the community, providing workshops and forums for discussion, as well as acting as a clearinghouse for all kinds of educational resources.

Still another type of legal entity is the 527, commonly known as a political action committee, or PAC. As I'm writing this, laws governing PACs are probably changing because they were so controversial during the 2004 presidential election. At least at this point, PACs are exempt from federal taxes *except* for any lobbying or other items not directly related to electing candidates to office.

You may decide that it makes sense to have more than one kind of organization, as we have done with D.C. Parents for School Choice, a 501(c)(4), and our sister organization, Parents for Educational Choices, Inc. Because the latter is a 501(c)(3) nonprofit, people can make tax-deductible donations that benefit either the program-oriented work of the 501(c)(3) or the advocacy work of the 501(c)(4).

My single most important piece of advice on this subject: *Be sure you talk with a qualified professional as you make this important decision and file all the applicable paperwork.* We have worked closely with an attorney and accountant to ensure that we follow the tax laws in everything we do, including keeping separate bank accounts, boards of directors, staff, and so on.*

Step 2. Develop Your Board of Directors

In the beginning, we started out by asking friends and family for money to support our cause. This was how we kept things going at first, but then we had to step up our efforts. Our greatest fundraising power ultimately came from our board of directors, so I suggest you take board development very seriously.

You might ask, *What about the parents?* They're central to every other effort in your organization, so why not have them help with fundraising, too? Some grassroots organizations take this approach, but I don't believe it's a good idea to have parents hold bake sales, solicit donations directly, or contribute their own money. It just doesn't sit well. What grown men and women want to be treated like Girl Scouts, who sell cookies as part of the troop's activities? Who wants to attend a meeting and feel ambushed, as if they were brought there on the pretext of school choice but are actually being pumped for cash? Not anyone I know.

If you're not going to rely on your membership for money, you have even more reasons to choose wisely when inviting people to participate as board members. The main responsibilities of the board of directors should be:

---

* For additional, general information on possible organizational structures, see the workbook, *Building the Base: A Blueprint for Grassroots Leaders in the School Choice Movement* by Donna Watson, pages 151–153.

✓ To help you articulate and refine the direction and goals of your organization

✓ To help you determine a sound strategy for achieving those goals (exact steps for implementing the strategy may be formally written down or informally agreed upon in conversation; either way, these steps are referred to as "policies")

✓ To help you develop the resources—such as personnel and funding—needed to implement the policies

Who will be good members of your board? Look to the prominent leaders in your area: Who has resources? Who is wealthy, wise, and unafraid of work? Who are the respected business, civic, and church leaders in your community? Who already cares about school choice and is willing to make a commitment to you and your organization? (If the parents are the "grass roots," who are the "grass tops"?)

When you invite people to become board members, do so with the explicit understanding that the three reasons listed above are why they'll be joining you. Board members are legally and financially responsible for the conduct of your nonprofit organization. Help them understand that they will be developing policies that require them to give personally, fundraise from others, donate their time for the cause, or give gifts-in-kind. (Note: Every state has its own laws about the minimum number of directors for a board, how often to meet, and how detailed the minutes of your meetings need to be. Be sure to check with a trusted attorney about the requirements in your area.)

On our board, we are fortunate to have both a lawyer and an accountant. They donate in-kind services—we get free legal and tax advice—as well as their time, expertise, and knowledge in board meetings. Every member of our board has made a significant cash contribution, and most have solicited funds from their colleagues and contacts on our behalf. This is exactly how your board can and should help you with fundraising.

<table>
<tr><td>

What Do *They* Care About?

You'll notice that my elevator speech didn't start with the buzzwords "school choice," "voucher program," or even "opportunity scholarships."

That's because some people perceive this is as a Republican issue and tune out as soon as you say those phrases. (For more on diffusing this misperception, see chapter 6.) D.C. is a Democratic city, most of my friends are Democrats, and it's important to talk with them first about something *they* care about, which is the fate of children in our public schools.

Remember what Martin Luther King, Jr. said: "**If you want to move people, it has to be toward a vision that's positive for them, that taps important values, that gets them something they desire, and it has to be presented in a compelling way that they feel inspired to follow.**"

Plan to do a lot of networking, focusing on talking to people about what *they* care about.

</td></tr>
</table>

Step 3. Remember, Money Is Not a Four-Letter Word

You will be a member of your own board, its executive director. In this role, you are just as responsible for fundraising as the other board members are, though you may approach it differently. For me, this meant talking about our organization in every possible setting, especially at social gatherings where people of means were in attendance. So, yes, I began to talk about our cause, and occasionally about the money we needed for it, in polite company. I learned to deliver an "elevator speech"—a thirty-second introduction to what we were doing. (The idea is that I could say this bit in the time it would take to ride an elevator from one floor to the next.) If someone's interest was piqued, then I'd be ready to tell more, including the story of my son William, which you've read several times in this book already.

All of this would be delivered briefly, so I wouldn't be foisting myself on someone. It would be more like cocktail chatter. Someone would say, "What do you do?"

I would respond, "Well, you know how badly our public schools are doing in D.C. right now? They're some of the worst in the nation in terms of test scores and violence. I'm working to create new options for low-income families and give their kids a second chance."

At that point, the person either wanted to know more, changed the subject, or was ready to head for the hors d'oeuvres and drinks. If he or she indicated an interest, I'd say something like, "The reason I'm involved in this is that my own son, William, was failing miserably in public schools. He was hanging out with a scary crowd, flunking out, getting in trouble with the police. Thank God, we were given a private scholarship to put him in a different school. I'm convinced that it changed his life. I believe he'd be either dead or on drugs now if this hadn't happened to us. William's a grown man today, and I'm working to make scholarships like this available to other families who can't afford to do what I did."

Still interested? I'd say, "Look, this is a party and I don't want to talk your ear off with this. If you want to know more, give me a call. There are lots of ways you can help us out—we're D.C. Parents for School Choice, and here's my card. May I have one of yours?"

Maybe they'd insist we talk more right then, which I was always happy to do, or they'd just take the card. Sometimes they'd say no and just walk away. Surprisingly, even this response sometimes led to a donation. One fellow gave us a check for $100 and told me, "I don't really support what you're doing, but I want to do something." This was probably because it was clear to him that children were being hurt, that they were being sacrificed to a broken system. Most people who don't agree with vouchers as a solution have never made the connection between the program and the children it will serve. They've never actually spoken with someone who can clarify how opportunity scholarships bring resources to people who otherwise have no hope. When they do, it becomes an entirely different issue for them.

Whether a person makes that connection right then or later on (or never), you make a new contact. Sometimes they'll take a few days then call back. If not, allow some time to pass, then give them a ring. "Remember me? From so-and-so's party? I'm just following up on our conversation. Would you like to talk about this some more and find out how you can help improve education options for low-income families in our area?"

If you want to extend the contact with someone you meet in a social situation, consider inviting them to a "meet and greet." Periodically, D.C. Parents for School Choice hosted get-togethers at African-American-owned coffee houses in D.C. for just this purpose. We'd invite the contacts I'd made and the board members' contacts, serve them coffee and pastries, and introduce them to the board members and a few parents who would volunteer to come and tell their stories. At the end of the evening, we didn't pass the hat, but we did say, "There are ways for you to help, through donations of money, time, or services. Please let us know what you're willing to do to improve education options for low-income families in D.C."

Step 4. Let Your Conscience Be Your Guide

Most of our donations were for individual projects or activities, and we even had sponsorships for fundraising activities like the meet and greets described above. (Someone had to pay for the coffee and pastries, right?) We relied on one donor in particular whenever we wanted to launch something with a significant price tag. Work to find a few champions like this whom you can call whenever you need seed money for a project you know will move your campaign forward in a significant way.

One of our biggest donors was Pat Rooney, an insurance company owner whose contributions kept us afloat more than once. It's also important to disclose to you that his business practices have been questioned in some circles. Let me tell you, I have known Mr. Rooney for many years, and although I don't know the particulars of his business dealings, his desire to help kids has always been completely sincere. His financial support of our group occasionally brought criticism our way, though, as if our taking money from him sullied us in some way. I say that's nonsense, not only because I know Mr. Rooney as a lovely man, but also because his donations had no strings attached.

It's important for you to be selective but not exclusive about where your money comes from. In other words, you need to be wise enough to know the difference between someone who may have an imperfect reputation and someone who will ask you to do something that goes against what you believe. Given the

> ### Examine Your Motives
>
> This simply can't be about money. It can't be about earning a salary. Nobody ever got rich (or even comfortable) through ethical grassroots organizing. To be completely frank, I'm poor as a church mouse, but thank God I'm blessed with a husband who makes a good salary. If Earl didn't pay the bills, I promise I couldn't do all this.
>
> If you don't have some form of financial support, whether it's from your own labor or family to help you, you need to carefully consider how you will manage this. There will be lean times and possibly lush times for your group, but you should not expect in any way, shape, or form to line your own pockets. Be sure you're doing the right thing for you, your family, and the organization.

political climate in which we operate, if you're willing to take money only from people who've never received bad press, you may find yourself with no funds at all. (You wouldn't be able to take my money, that's for sure.) At the same time, you must be vigilant in protecting your own sense of what's "good money" and "bad money."

Here's an example. At one point in our campaign, we became prominent enough in the school choice movement that donors and other people with resources we needed started coming to us unsolicited. In fact, someone contacted us to make an anonymous donation of $250,000. Fantastic! We definitely needed the money, we arranged for the funds to arrive, and we were set to begin some new programs that had badly needed funding.

Two months later, after about half of the money was spent, our anonymous donor's representative called and asked me to do and say some things having to do with universal vouchers, which I don't support. Instead, I sent them a check for the remaining amount. They were shocked! Wouldn't our cash-strapped little organization do anything for money? No, it wouldn't.

I can't be bought. Don't allow yourself to get suckered into doing anything you don't believe in just for cash, either. It's simply not worth it personally. It's doesn't really benefit your organization, anyway. How much influence, integrity, and credibility would a grassroots organization for sale to the highest bidder really have? Not much. You have to let your conscience, and the trust of the people you represent, drive the direction of the organization.

Focus on finding contributors who already believe in what you're doing. It's worthy! You don't have to become anything other than what you already are. The parents who've placed their faith in you, and the children whose futures depend on you, know that. They also know there are more important things in life than money, and you're one of them.

5

Foster a Capitol Idea:
Taking Your Program through the Legislature

"I've come to the conclusion that parents and students who are stuck in under-performing schools need—no, have the right to choose from a wider pool. I have received calls from parents who are frustrated, angry, and even emotionally distraught by the condition of their child's school. It's time to do more than sympathize. This is a moral imperative."
From the statement of Representative Tom Davis (R-Va.) during the Government Reform Committee Hearing, June 24, 2003

After a yearlong heated battle, in early 2004 the U.S. Senate approved the three-sector bill, which at last provided $14 million in private scholarships to low-income parents in D.C., as well as equal funding to the District's public and charter schools.[†] It would never have arrived on the Senate floor if Dianne Feinstein had not cast her deciding vote in a crucial hearing. Without her, the bill would have died. Up until then, Feinstein had shown consistent opposition, yet she changed her mind when the mayor stood up in support for school choice in the District.

No doubt Mayor Anthony Williams was also influenced by the opinions of other high-profile, local Democrats. The president of D.C.'s board of education, Peggy Cooper Cafritz, and D.C. City Council member Kevin Chavous, among others,

---

[†] To read the entire text of the *D.C. School Choice Incentive Act of 2003,* turn to appendix E, "The Legislation That Passed."

had recently become voucher-friendly. The local effort turned a corner at a key meeting, influenced in large part by Chavous's fellow council member, David Catania.

What set this domino effect in motion and ultimately led to victory for us in Congress?

Part of it was the dire situation in D.C.: Our schools were considered some of the worst, with per-student spending among the highest while test scores remained the lowest in the nation. The average D.C. SAT score was 799, yet the national average was 1,020. The dropout rate was 40 percent in the District. The number of assaults, both those considered "simple" and those with deadly weapons, was rising sharply in D.C. schools, as was the number of students bringing concealed weapons to school.

I don't believe these facts alone made the difference. Our faces made the problem real and our voices demanded a solution.

Nothing gets the attention of elected officials like a groundswell of support for an issue. There are two things at work here: the idealism and the ambition that gets people into politics in the first place. If you can appeal to both the values of a politician and his or her desire to continue to hold office, then you have a lever that can move mountains.

This, of course, is the whole reason you form a grassroots organization: to let the people in power know what you want and that you won't rest until you get it. Our strategy from the beginning was to get parents and other people in the community involved and visible in the fight. As you read in chapter 3, large numbers of committed citizens attract media attention. At some point, vocal, persistent, dedicated people also attract the attention of politicians, primarily because elected representatives can't afford to ignore their constituencies.

More than once, campaign leaders told me that if it had not been for our group, they would never have been able to influence Congress. If it had not been for the grassroots support of parents, they would not have been so willing to fight. They needed to know they had the people behind them.

Be Prepared for the Twists and Turns

Don't let this quick description of our success fool you. In truth, the District considered, argued, and postured on vouchers for nearly a decade before it finally acted. A bill made it through both houses of Congress in 1997, only to be vetoed by President Clinton. In 2001, legislation was introduced to provide scholarships for ten states, but it was defeated in the Senate. The debate heated up and cooled off several times, but there was never a year that went by when some of us didn't get together to strategize and plan for victory. Things really came to a boil in February 2003, when Representative Jeff Flake (R-Ariz.) introduced H.R. 684, a new school choice bill just for the District. Sparked by this promising legislation, D.C. Parents for School Choice made its most consistent, vigilant, and determined effort yet—and sustained it for ten grueling months. During that time, the sponsors and legislation changed, but ultimately we won $14 million in opportunity scholarships for the District's low-income families.

This book focuses primarily on our final push of the campaign, but I want to be completely candid about it being a much longer and larger struggle. Some states may adopt voucher legislation quickly, yet it's all relative. In my experience, one year would be an accelerated campaign. It's much more typical for voucher activists to experience many, many ups and downs, wins and losses, before they see a school choice bill become law. In Maryland, we worked for two years to get a bill through the state legislature to start public charter schools. Polly Williams led her parent group in Milwaukee for a year before the voucher legislation was passed there. And seven years after Cleveland instituted a school choice program, parents were still active in its advocacy and defense when its constitutionality was challenged in the U.S. Supreme Court. (I'll give you more information on what has to be done *after* the legislation passes, to ensure the security of your voucher program, in chapter 8, "Free at Last.")

At the height of a campaign, the schedule can be rigorous, but it's entirely necessary. During those last ten months in 2003 in the District, in addition to serving the community, listening to the needs of the parents, recruiting people to help with the cause, training them in how to present their stories, and keeping them informed about the education issues in their area . . .

- ✓ We visited Capitol Hill every day. Every morning at 10 A.M., I arrived with about twenty-five parents to walk the halls, show our faces, and meet with legislators.

- ✓ We wore our D.C. Parents for School Choice T-shirts so there was no mistaking us for tourists—anyone who saw us knew we meant business.

- ✓ We stopped in to talk with legislators in their offices.

- ✓ We went to every hearing relative to the bill we supported.

- ✓ I met regularly with the authors of the legislation to keep them up to date on our activities and to offer my opinions and support.

- ✓ Parents attended press conferences with the legislators.

- ✓ I went to the Hill anytime anyone was talking about anything to do with education.

We developed our strategy alongside the legislators who had written the various bills, in coordination with the D.C. Coalition. We conferred with one another: commiserated, collaborated, and cooperated. We advised each other about what we were doing and what should come next. Toward the end, our parent group was practically on call, wanting to be present whenever steps were being taken to further our cause. We were about as common a sight on the Hill as the Capitol itself.

How Your State's Campaign Will Be Different—and the Same

From state to state, the issues that give rise to the need for education reform differ, the public school systems may have unique challenges, and the demographics and psychographics of the parents in each area may vary, as well. Yet the campaigns themselves are remarkably the same. When I assisted with the effort in Maryland, I was struck by how similar it was to what we were doing in D.C. In Maryland, we had to cover more geography, our parent leaders served districts rather than neighborhoods, and we had to deal with the logistics of transporting some people long distances instead of across town. Some of the "practicals" changed because of the size of the state, but all of the principles were the same.

There was one key difference. In D.C., we had a unique political climate to deal with, specifically because the people we had to

---

How a Bill Becomes a Law

Each state has its own legislative process, though most base theirs on the federal system. Following is a refresher course on how a bill becomes a law at the national level.

First reading. Any member of Congress may introduce legislation (a bill). He or she gives it to the clerk of the Senate or House of Representatives (whichever one he or she belongs to), and after this "first reading," it's given a number, then referred to the proper committee.

Table or hearings. The committee can kill the bill right away if it doesn't find it worthy of discussion (thus "tabling" it), or it can decide to send the bill for a "hearing," where facts and opinions are presented on the bill. Members of the committee can offer changes (amendments), and then the bill is brought to a vote. If the majority vote yea, then the bill goes back to the floor of the House or Senate—or possibly to another committee for further study and debate.

Second reading. The clerk reads the bill, line by line,

Continued on next page.

"How a Bill Becomes a Law," continued

to the members of the House or Senate who are present during the session. Members can then debate further and offer amendments. In the House, there is a time limit for debate, but in the Senate, there is not, opening the door to a filibuster, wherein Senators stall the next step by making lengthy presentations.

Third reading. Next, the clerk reads the title of the bill only, and it is put to a vote.

If the bill passes, it goes to the other house of Congress. (Bills that start in the Senate move to the House, and vice versa.) In committee, it may be defeated, amended, or brought back to the floor for a final vote. If it is passed with amendments, a joint committee of Congress is formed to arrive at an acceptable compromise.

If a bill passes in both houses of Congress, it goes to the president for signature. The president may veto, thus killing the bill, or sign, thus making it law. If the president doesn't wish either to sign or veto, the bill can be held for

Continued on next page.

persuade to support our bill were not from this area and, in fact, were not our elected officials. The District of Columbia is governed by the U.S. Congress rather than a state house and senate. Because of this, we faced apathy about our situation that I hope you will not have to confront. It was frequently difficult to get the attention of members of Congress who didn't want to put their time or energy into legislation that wouldn't directly affect constituencies in their home states.

Yet I always considered our efforts in D.C. emblematic. It's our nation's capital, a fishbowl, the absolute best place to innovate and create new options in education. What we do here affects what happens all over the country. If you think about it that way, then you can conclude that Congress is responsible for what kind of picture is presented to all of its citizens. If D.C. doesn't work, supposedly run by some of the finest minds in the country, what does that say about the entire nation?

You can see why the backing of the mayor and other

prominent local citizens—as well as the strong presence of our parents on the Hill—was particularly important in gaining the consideration and support of people who were busy serving their own constituencies. Indeed, during one hearing, Senator Feinstein recognized that if the mayor was in support of vouchers, and if the public schools were failing

"How a Bill Becomes a Law," continued

ten days. If Congress adjourns during that time, the bill is killed in what's called a "pocket veto." If Congress remains in session, the bill automatically becomes a law without signature.

so miserably to meet the needs of low-income families, then it was Congress's duty as national representatives to take up the cause and enact legislation that would address the problem. This was, as I mentioned, the tipping point in our campaign that led directly to the bill going to the Senate floor for a vote.

Despite this unusual added dynamic, as we talked with individual legislators, we encountered much the same kind of concerns, resistance, and outright opposition that I expect you will. We heard all of the usual comments: "This legislation will benefit only a small number of families," "This is just a way for public money to fund private religious schools," and "This is taking much-needed money away from public schools." I'll give you some of my responses to these and other criticisms in the next chapter to help you deal with political pressures, but when we visited with legislators, we didn't go to stage a debate. Instead, our real goal in meeting with them was always to make the necessity for vouchers real, to put a face on the problem, to help them see why this is a priority. Again, the parents' stories took center stage.

In fact, we once dropped by the office of the chair of the House Appropriations Committee, Representative Rodney Frelinghuysen (R-N.J.). The committee was getting ready to vote on the amount of money to be given to the voucher program, and we'd stopped in, again, to reinforce how important this was

63

to the parents of D.C. To our delight, he sat down with us and asked to hear more about how this would affect low-income families. Some parents talked about how scholarships had made the difference for their children; some talked about how their kids were struggling in public schools without any options for making a change—each describing a very personal event in a succinct, moving testimonial to the positive impact of vouchers. What a wonderful surprise! Just before he walked out the door to help determine how much would be granted to this program we'd worked so hard to get passed, Frelinghuysen heard nearly fifty powerful stories from impassioned parents. The committee came back with a sum of $10 million for D.C. parents and children.‡

Develop Your Own Political Savvy

Democracy at work is inspiring and impressive. Some of the behind-the-scenes business can be less so. As the leader of your organization, you will probably see some of what most people think of when they hear the word *politics:* power brokering, wheeling and dealing, special interests. Your parents will not see, nor should they be subjected to, the backroom conversations that will occur among lobbyists and elected officials. Remember that politicians are often lawyers, and even when they aren't, they fully understand negotiation and its role in getting the best possible deal for their "clients," who are their constituents and, in some cases, their financial backers.

In the beginning, this was what I found most shocking: Politicians are willing to barter for votes. This is not illegal, nor is it unethical; it's just how the job gets done. For an idealist like me, it definitely took me aback. Compromises were made, votes

---

‡ Later, when the bill was reworked for presentation to the Senate, the amount increased to $14 million.

were secured by offering support for someone else's cause, and this was all in a day's work.

We gave things up in our campaign that I wish we could have kept, but that doesn't mean I believe we should have stuck to our guns. It's important to be willing to compromise in some instances, as long as it gets you closer to your ultimate objective. Here's an example: When Mayor Williams decided to give his support to the campaign, there was discussion among the school choice advocates, including some legislators, lobbyists, and me. Up until then, the proposed legislation had included provisions for parents who live in D.C. to use vouchers to put their kids in any private school, and many parents had hoped to move their kids to nearby Maryland and Virginia schools. The mayor was opposed to having any of the money for a D.C. voucher program leave the District, and he wanted that possibility explicitly excluded. This was clearly a sticking point for him.

As for me, I was crushed. Many members of D.C. Parents for School Choice would not benefit from the legislation if this was how it proceeded. These were, as you are now well aware, people who had become dear to me, who had worked hard, freely giving their time to the cause. They were people I had literally laughed and cried with for years. Yet it was obvious that the mayor would withdraw his support if we didn't get on board to keep the money inside the boundaries of the District. When the group asked for my opinion, I quietly acquiesced, then went home to give the most difficult talk I've ever delivered to the parents.

Although less emotionally draining, we made another, more significant compromise. I mentioned earlier that Flake's initial D.C. voucher legislation had lit a fire under my parent group, and when the Boehner-Davis version passed in the House, we were on cloud nine. Shortly thereafter, though, the decision was made to rework the bill for presentation to the Senate because it was clear that a win there would require some concessions and

additions. This was when our voucher legislation turned into the
three-sector bill, sponsored by Senators Judd Gregg (R-N.H.) and
Michael DeWine (R-Ohio), providing money not only for low-
income parents desiring school choice, but also giving equal
amounts to public and charter schools. It was a move to pacify
the public school advocates who would try to block the bill, plus
it was an answer to the concern of public funds benefiting a
small number of students. Although I could see the wisdom of
this strategy, it definitely rankled. First, D.C. public schools
enjoyed the highest amount of per-student funding already and
were performing dismally despite it; and second, giving those
failing schools even more money removed any possible
competitive incentive that the vouchers might have created.

So I went back to this group of parents, still high from their
victory in the House, to tell them we had a change of plans. I
had to let them know that, although I personally did not support
giving more money to the public schools (incidentally, I had no
beef with better funding for charter schools, which were doing
remarkably well on one-third of the public school budget), this
was the best strategy for getting our voucher program through
the Senate. As usual, the parents were committed to the big
picture. They had their moment of disappointment but then
marched on.

One of the great things about leading a grassroots
organization is that none of its members need to give much
energy or attention to the political maneuvering. Leave that to
the politicians. As the group's leader, prepare yourself to see
negotiations that might make your hair stand on end and to
carry messages to the parents that you'd rather not. At the same
time, remember to keep everyone focused on getting your voices
heard—that's where you'll be most effective.

This effort is personal and political, practical and romantic.
You are taking your heartfelt desires for your own family and
friends and bringing them into the public arena where they can

improve the lives of people you've never even met. You are engaging in incredibly hard work while holding onto the patriotic ideal of "we, the people" as the ones who will form a more perfect union.

It makes me think of *Mr. Smith Goes to Washington*, which is one of my favorite movies, not because he won in the end, but because he was a regular person who had something to say and got this incredible opportunity to say it. You don't have to be a senator to do that. You speak up because what you think makes a difference. Yes, it's romantic, but that doesn't mean it's not real, too. I watched the members of D.C. Parents for School Choice grow from people who were loving and caring, who wanted to make a difference in their own children's lives, into incredibly empowered women and men who knew to the very core of their being that what they were doing was right. That's both humbling and ennobling. That's power to the people. That's democracy in action.

6

Stay Focused:
Dealing with Political Pressures

"Vouchers and other tax-diversion proposals are a pernicious, steal-from-the-poor-and-give-to-the-rich scheme. They would take money from our public school students, give it instead to private schools, and abandon many of our children in the process."
—*Kweisi Mfume, former NAACP executive director, quoted in a news release from People for the American Way Foundation, February 13, 1998*

In one hearing, members of the Congressional Black Caucus stood up and called D.C. Parents for School Choice, and anyone else who was black and in favor of vouchers, "stupid," "brainwashed," and "puppets of the right." I can't remember a time when I felt more upset than when men and women who looked like me, who shared my commitment to racial equality, and whom I respected as political leaders, condescended to us and condemned our cause as suspect and unworthy of our race.

In other contexts, I have been dismissed as a "darling of the right," as well as called an "operative," "pirate," and the mouthpiece for a bunch of white conservatives. Some days, I find this amusing. Who can get mad picturing herself as some adorable spy with a parrot and eye patch? Other days, I feel like screaming to anyone who will listen that the only people I speak for are myself, the parents in my organization, and their children. At other times, I just put my head in my hands and cry.

Throughout this book, I counsel you to get thick-skinned but I don't suppose anything I write will prepare you for an unexpected and vicious verbal assault. The day of that rough-and-tumble hearing, I gathered up the parents and walked out of the gallery, mainly because I knew that if it was affecting me this deeply, surely they were hurting and angry, too. I figured it was only a matter of time before someone did something disruptive, just because I don't think any group would find it possible to sit through such bile without some comment, whether in the form of tears or tirade. In fact, we lost parents from our organization that day, dear people who told me they just couldn't take it anymore.

This chapter is about preparing you for both the polite debate and the rude assault of politics. Those who oppose school choice are often intelligent, compassionate individuals convinced of the rightness of their position. There are also those who are not above misconstruing the facts (or being stubbornly ignorant of them), attempting to manipulate public perception, or insulting you in an effort to shut down your efforts.

There are many examples, but here's one that I still find astonishing. Several parents once came to me to report a rumor that school choice activism in the District was merely a ruse for collecting personal data on poor families, and that no vouchers would ever be delivered. Incredulous, when I checked this out, I discovered that the lie had come out of a teachers' organization.

Indeed, the teachers' unions and other public school advocates believe they have the most to lose when it comes to vouchers. Because most public schools receive federal funding on a per-student basis, leaders of these organizations persuade their members to fear the impact of vouchers on their job security, respect in the classroom, and public education in general. (It's important to note here, of course, that many teachers see through the machinations of the unions and do not oppose school choice.) In this chapter, you'll see how these are false concerns and that most public schools actually benefit by having a voucher program in their district.

Both the National Education Association (NEA) and the American Federation of Teachers (AFT), the two most powerful teachers' unions, have staunch positions against vouchers, and their influence is felt far beyond the classroom. Legislators in the Democratic Party are frequently backed by teachers' unions, so it makes sense that they would fight for these organizations' interests.

Add to that the history of segregation, and black Democrats can be particularly vehement in their opposition to vouchers, which move some of the poorest students, who are usually from minority races, out of public schools. Then put one more fly in the ointment: Most of the champions of school choice are white Republicans. In this chapter, you'll gain further insight into this racial tension and a viewpoint that can help you defuse it.

Civil liberties organizations also get into the fray because many private schools are associated with religion. Constitutionality becomes an issue—and again, I'll address that concern and show you how school choice clearly adheres to the First Amendment.

So you'll have a quick reference, I've organized this chapter by what I perceive to be the false assertions of those who oppose school choice, and followed each with what I know to be true. My intention is that by unveiling the opposition, you will be in a better position to stay focused when things get rocky. If you know what's coming, and you share this information with the parents in your organization, you can support one another through even the most heated public and private disagreements.

False Assertion #1: *Voucher programs take needed money away from public schools.*

This was especially untrue in D.C. In other scholarship programs, school districts don't receive money for children they no longer serve — a reasonable position to most people. Under the three-sector bill, D.C. public schools still receive money for children it no longer serves: $14 million was earmarked for the public schools, plus another $14 million for charter schools. Far from draining money, this scholarship program is a windfall for the school district.

In other states, the public schools don't fare much worse:

✓ According to the recent state audit of the Milwaukee Parental Choice Program, "During the period in which the Choice program has been funded Milwaukee Public Schools experienced a net increase in both equalization aid and total state aids." Further, since the start of the program, public school enrollment in Milwaukee rose 8 percent, spending rose 29 percent, and state aid to Milwaukee public schools increased 55 percent.

✓ In Florida, the seventy-eight government schools given an "F" grade will receive more than $47 million in additional federal and state funds, and the 613 schools given a "D" grade will receive more than $284 million. Moreover, according to Governor Jeb Bush, "per-student spending in public schools will remain the same regardless of the number of students who use Opportunity Scholarships."

✓ In Cleveland, public schools still receive per-pupil funds for students enrolled in the voucher program. In 1997, this meant that the revenue received by the Cleveland Public Schools was actually $118,000 more than the entire cost of the voucher program.

✓ Finally, since the programs in Minnesota and Arizona are based on individual income taxes, they do not directly affect money set aside for public schools.

Conclusion: School choice does not drain money from public schools. Instead, it allows public schools to use their money to educate students more effectively.

False Assertion #2: *The use of vouchers is unconstitutional under the First Amendment separation of church and state.*

School choice programs have been upheld in various courts of law, declaring them constitutional.

In determining whether a program violates the First Amendment, the U.S. Supreme Court primarily uses the precedent set by the 1971 *Lemon v. Kurtzman* decision. The so-called Lemon Test says that, to ensure the separation of church and state, a program must have a secular purpose, which in the case of vouchers is the education of all children. In addition, no program aiding sectarian institutions can have the "primary effect" of advancing religion or result in "excessive entanglement" between church and state.

In 1998–99, the U.S Supreme Court upheld a federally funded program to provide remedial instruction by public school teachers at religious schools, and let stand decisions by the Wisconsin and Arizona Supreme Courts upholding vouchers and tax credits, respectively.

Conclusion: When an individual uses public funds to make a private choice—in this case when a parent uses a voucher to make an individual decision to send his or her children to a public, private, or religious school—it does not violate the First Amendment.

False Assertion #3: *This is just a ploy by religious schools to get public funding.*

Parents with vouchers decide where to send their children to school, not the other way around. They make this choice based on the needs of their children. Usually, it has more to do with academics than religion.

73

In the District, about half of the private schools are religious. In other parts of the nation, the ratio is different. I don't believe any voucher program would force parents to choose religious schools for their children.

I know that with my own son, whom I placed in a Catholic school, I was more concerned with his safety than anything else. (Incidentally, my family attends a Methodist church.) I was not alone: One out of five parents, when asked what their priority is for the children they place in a private school on a voucher, answer that it is safety.

Anyone who is concerned that religious schools are conspiring in some way to enact opportunity scholarships, such as recruiting parents to advocate for this cause, need only talk to the parents in any grassroots organization. It's simply not true. Parents are involved in this movement because they desperately need better choices for their children

Conclusion: Parents, not religious schools, drive the voucher movement.

False Assertion #4: *Private schools are not accountable in terms of hiring practices, discrimination against students, or the use of money they receive from public sources.*

Not true. In D.C., any low-income child can apply for a scholarship, and admissions are decided by lotteries. For hiring, the law allows discrimination based on religion so religious schools aren't forced to hire people hostile to their faith.

Under law, participating private schools are held accountable, both financially and academically, by the Department of Education.

Furthermore, private schools depend entirely upon students' parents for funding. If parents decide they do not agree with a school's policies, they can withdraw the student and place him or her elsewhere.

Conclusion: Private schools answer to the most important group of all: the parents.

False Assertion #5: *Voucher programs serve only a small number of students.*

In D.C., the scholarships are part of a comprehensive, three-sector plan, which also provides funds to revitalize public schools.

What's more, public schools pay attention when school choice is on the table, when parents have an option. This competition is healthy for the schools and beneficial for all students. In Milwaukee, Cleveland, San Antonio, Florida, and Albany, school choice has had a positive impact on public schools, including boosting new teacher hiring and providing additional resources to students. For example, the Milwaukee Public School Board, in addition to closing six schools identified as failing, now guarantees that they will teach kids to read by the second grade or provide a tutor. In Albany, the introduction of private vouchers for every child in Geffen Elementary School led the school board to replace the principal, hire new teachers, and set aside $125,000 for books, equipment, and teacher training. Parents I've talked with say this has made a positive difference.

In addition, vouchers are just a beginning. There's no question that they do not solve all the problems of public schools, and they're not designed to. They're intended to address the needs of those who are most likely to get crushed under the wheels of a broken system. If nothing else, vouchers start the

> **Help as Many as We Can**
>
> Can you imagine if I had said to my neighbor, who offered my son a scholarship to a better school, "If you can't give money to all the kids in the neighborhood, I don't want your help"? Nether can I. We have a responsibility to help as many children as we can, whether that means giving a modest number of families much-needed vouchers or motivating the school districts to better performance through competition.

dialogue about why public schools are failing and what needs to be done to improve them.

Conclusion: Public schools need all the help they can get, and they've proven responsive to competition.

False Assertion #6: *Grassroots voucher groups populated by low-income black parents are just fronts for a white, conservative agenda.*

If I thought anyone was using me and the parents I lead to promote their ideas, I wouldn't be in this fight. I'm not a person who can be told what to do. If I didn't think vouchers would be effective in helping my community gain greater educational freedom, I simply wouldn't participate. I think most activists who are black and in this movement feel the same way.

I'm a pragmatist. It doesn't really matter who else is in this movement with me. So long as kids are being served, and I'm not being asked to say or do anything I don't already believe in, I don't really care about my colleagues' skin color or political party.

I'm sure there are folks who are funding this effort who don't share my motives, and there are people in this movement who don't share my views. For example, I don't support universal vouchers, or any voucher program that's not mean-tested; I only support vouchers that support low-income families, those who don't have any real choices right now. We agree to disagree, and as long as they don't ask me to advocate something I don't believe in, we live and let live.

This idea that I'm working with some Machiavellian puppet masters trying to pull my strings and make me dance to their tune is just false. Most of the men and women I've met who advocate this needed change have a sincere desire to make life better for parents and kids. We work together because we want some of the same things. We have mutual respect, shared goals, occasional differences of opinion, and a commitment to improving the educational opportunities for all children in this country.

Conclusion: Black parents represent themselves, not anyone else.

False Assertion #7: *School choice is a Republican issue.*

This effort is championed and funded in large part by Republicans, so there is a stereotyped misperception that it is a solution favored only by fat cats who want to make big bucks in private schools. In truth, this issue is complicated by politics but clear as day when you actually walk into a school. Anyone who takes the time to visit a classroom, walk on a campus, talk with parents, or spend some time with students gets a rude awakening to the reality of D.C. public schools, and I'm sure it would be the same in your area. In the face of that reality, political parties seem pretty trivial.

It took serious courage for the local Democrats in D.C. to go against their political party and come out in favor of opportunity scholarships. Mayor Williams and Councilman Chavous took heavy criticism, and Chavous was not reelected. Many people think it's because he supported the voucher bill here. When he did so, he proved that the question of quality education cuts across party lines.

Conclusion: This is a bipartisan issue for anyone willing to look at the failure of public school education and to find solutions that will work for students today.

False Assertion #8: *School choice creates de facto segregation.*

School choice actually does the opposite. According to researcher Jay P. Greene, "analyses of a national sample of twelfth graders collected by the U.S. Department of Education show that private school students are more likely to be in racially mixed classes than are public school students."

In addition, Greene and Nicole Mellow point out that 63 percent of private school students observed in a lunchroom setting (where children could choose their own seats) were sitting in an integrated setting, compared to 49.7 percent of public school students.

The voucher program in Cleveland proves this point. Almost 20 percent of voucher recipients attend private schools that resemble the racial composition of the Cleveland metropolitan area, while only 5.2 percent of children in public schools are in similarly integrated schools. Also, 60.7 percent of public school students in the Cleveland metropolitan area attend schools that have either more than 90 percent white enrollment or fewer than 10 percent white enrollment.

Conclusion: Students in school choice programs are more likely to experience racial diversity in their schools.

False Assertion #9: *Given their history, vouchers are inherently racist.*

Yes, it's been fewer than a hundred years since the number of black kids in public schools finally equaled the number in private schools—and even fewer since blacks came to share the same and equal facilities as whites.

Yes, racists once used school vouchers to evade the 1954 *Brown v. Board of Education* decision, fleeing public schools to segregated private ones.

Yes, schools in a few states were shut down in defiance of the Brown decision, and many black families found themselves sending their kids away to relatives in other states, educating their children in makeshift schools and at home, or foregoing their children's education altogether because of it.

And yes, it can be difficult to subtract this history from the discussion about school vouchers today. Believe me, I know. I remember the marches, the fights, the riots, the police actions. We were in the middle of it all. My family was friends with the

families of the Little Rock Nine who integrated Central High.
By the time I attended that school a few years after they'd
graduated, I was called "nigger" nearly every day there, and not
just by the students. The number of black kids in our school felt
like a drop in the bucket, but we stuck it out. I actually begged
my daddy to let me go back to my old school, but he insisted I
stay because the resources and opportunities available there so far
outshone what we could get in an all-black school—and because
he knew we were paving the way for others to come. Those days
definitely firmed my backbone.

When segregationist politicians blocked schoolhouse
entrances, they wanted to keep minority children out to deny
them a quality education. Today, as anti-voucher politicians
block schoolhouse exits, they want to keep minority children
in—again denying them a quality education, condemning them
to a life of lost opportunities and unfulfilled dreams.

We need to look at what is in the best interest of kids now.
My own mother, who marched and taught in the first
desegregated schools, had to see it with her own eyes to believe
it. When she walked onto a campus in disrepair, talked with
teachers who were burned out and disillusioned, and observed
how aggressive and frightened the students were, she
acknowledged the truth about public schools today. This is *not*
what we fought for.

We didn't fight just to get our children into the building. We
fought to get our kids into a place that would best meet their
needs, where they could take advantage of all the things that
come with schools that are well funded. Now we need to fight
for those same things, and for learning environments that are
free from violence.

The politicians must step away from the doors, and let our
children go.

Lack of school choice is a new kind of segregation, one based
on economics. Affluent parents have choices about where their

kids attend school, while poor parents have none. Vouchers help to address this inequity.

Conclusion: Vouchers offer freedom from economic segregation to low-income families.

These nine statements and responses encapsulate the political arguments as they stand today. For additional information on the pro-voucher position, please refer to appendix B, "Key Studies to Support School Choice."

In your area, you may have even more specific opposition to address. The American Education Reform Foundation (SchoolChoiceInfo.org) published a "point/counter-point" list for us to give parents, detailing what our local delegate to the House of Representatives, Eleanor Holmes Norton (D-D.C.), was saying about the voucher effort, and our rebuttal, a position shared by Mayor Anthony Williams. I've included a copy of this information at the end of this chapter. Consider creating something like this for your parents, too, and know that you'll probably have to update it from time to time.

No doubt there will new challenges to voucher programs in the years to come. No doubt this will present new opportunities for us to refine and redefine our position. I welcome the continuing dialogue.

Am I always excited and ready to engage in debate with opponents about the promise of opportunity scholarships? Mostly I am, but there are days when I feel nervous about speaking out, because I'm regularly attacked for my views, and some days I just don't want to deal with it. Then I go to a meeting with parents in the community, and I see the kids who are attending school on opportunity scholarships—their eyes are bright, reflecting how happy and enthusiastic they are now. For me, that makes it worth it.

When you feel daunted or dragged down by the political disputes over this issue, I suggest you go and look into the children's faces. Stop and ask your parents to do the same. This is where all the answers live and breathe. Those kids embody all hope and every reason to continue the fight.

Sample Argument Summary

Point/Counter-Point
The Debate Over K-12 Scholarships for D.C.

Representative Eleanor Holmes Norton, the National Education Association, and People for the American Way have been circulating "10 Reasons Why I Oppose D.C. Vouchers."

This document addresses each of their 10 points. When you consider the facts, we believe you'll decide it's time to give D.C. parents a choice, so their children can have a chance.

10 Reasons Why Eleanor Holmes Norton Opposes K-12 Scholarships for D.C.	Why D.C. Mayor Anthony Williams Wants You to Support D.C. School Choice
1. We must continue to support public money for public schools ONLY! There should be no appropriation of federal funds towards an unproven private school voucher program.	Shouldn't Congress care more about *whether* children get educated than *where* they go to school? If your children weren't thriving in their school, wouldn't you want more school options?
2. A congressional GAO (General Accounting Office) study of all the voucher jurisdictions has found no difference in student performance between students in public schools and students using private school vouchers.	That's not really what the GAO study found. The GAO report concludes that more research and programs (like one in D.C.) are needed. D.C. parents want more school options. The mayor thinks that's better for D.C. children, and he thinks a little competition would help improve the public system.

3. The majority of elected officials and residents in D.C. are on record opposing private school vouchers.	Sure, Representative Norton opposes the program. But the people mainly responsible for D.C. schools favor it. That includes the mayor, the D.C. School Board President, the Chairman of the D.C. City Council's Education Committee Chair.
4. A voucher program in D.C. would only serve 2, 000 of the 68,000 D.C. students. All of our children deserve a high quality education, not just a few.	The scholarships are part of a comprehensive, three-sector plan, which also provides funds to revitalize public schools. But, if Congress can set aside more money for scholarships, even better. More options for low-income families would mean more pressure on D.C. schools to improve.
5. Private schools are not accountable for the public monies they receive.	Under this law, participating private schools would be held accountable, both financially and academically, by DOE. It's true that the program won't regulate private schools like public schools. But that's a good thing.
6. Private schools are not prohibited from discriminating in their hiring and admission practices.	Not true. Any low-income child in D.C. can apply for a scholarship, and admissions will be decided by lotteries. For hiring, the law would allow discrimination based on religion so religious schools won't be forced to hire people hostile to their faith.
7. Private school vouchers will take millions of dollars from public schools. Especially today, when local schools have had their budgets cut, we do not want to see a competition begin between public and private school funding.	In other scholarship programs, school districts don't receive money for children they no longer serve—a reasonable position to most people. But for this program, DCPS still gets money for children it no longer serves. Far from draining money, this scholarship program is a windfall for the school district.

8. Two thousand students leaving D.C. Public Schools would mean the loss of $25 million from our public school system.	Again, not true. DCPS will be much better off financially with this program. DCPS is held harmless, even though it will serve fewer children.
9. Public dollars should be put into our public schools so that proven reform that serves all D.C. Public School students can be administered.	First, public dollars should be put into public *education,* not necessarily public *schools.* Second, school choice *is* a proven reform. Look at Milwaukee and other school choice programs to see how giving parents more options can improve a system.
10. D.C. already has school choice with its charter schools and transformation schools.	Charter schools and transformation schools are great, and the mayor's education plan supports them. But they only begin to satisfy the demand among low-income families for more school options.

7

Keep On Keeping On:
Seeing Persistence Pay

"From the richest person to the poorest person, we all want a good education for our children. We want our children to succeed. And most parents would say, 'I want my child to have a better education than I did, and I hope my child becomes something great.'

"I didn't have any hope for my kids before the scholarship fund was available. In the past, we never had a choice: It was make it or don't make it, especially among low-income parents, whether you had one child or seven.

"Thank God we have a choice now. I can leave my children in public schools, I can put them into charter schools or some other alternative school, and I can apply to put them into a private school. *We have a choice.*

"If a child can get the right education, God knows where that child can go in life."

—*Joseph Kelley, Jr., legal guardian of four children attending D.C. private schools on scholarships*

Throughout this book, I've laid it on the line for you: The challenges you and the parents will face in this fight can make you want to throw in the towel. You may find yourself exhausted and upset, as I often did, or in some other state of deeply felt emotion. The secret to staying in, even when you're weary, bleary, and beaten down, is to remember to go

85

back to the well and fill yourself up again with the hope and dreams of the people whose lives you're working to improve.

From the time we started our campaign, about three thousand parents have gotten involved in activities with D.C. Parents for School Choice. Among them, the parent leadership group—the individuals described in the first chapter—contributed the most to the stick-to-it-iveness of our effort. They did so much more than I can even say. Not only were they the backbone of all the work we did, but we were one another's emotional support, too. These were the people I could lean on. Be sure that you surround yourself with people who care about you, whom you can trust, who will listen to your own fears and aspirations and keep your confidences. These are your lieutenants, the people who will keep you going when you feel as if you're running out of steam. You'll find that your greatest strength comes from your relationships with these people and your shared goal to serve the rest of the community.

At this point, you don't need me to give you a motivational pep talk. If you've come this far, I suspect you're either in or out. You've probably made up your mind about whether you're cut out for this job of organizing parents. Assuming you're up to the challenge, the purpose of this chapter is to give you another place to come to fill up. So I want to end it by returning to the heart of school choice: the parents and kids who benefit most from these efforts. Here are a few more real stories told by real people in the District. These are about families who fought for and won the right to choose where their children would attend school. They are the reason I kept going. I hope they inspire you in the same way.

No More Drama

When my youngest was still in public school, he would complain to me about how mean the teachers were to him and how they didn't like him. In my opinion, because of the amount of time teachers spend with kids, they are helping to raise them, so it's important to me that my kids have a good relationship with their teachers. This just didn't seem possible for my kids in their schools—until we received the scholarships and were able to move them to private schools.

I see a difference in both of my boys now. The work they were doing before I moved them was below grade level. This year, though, my thirteen-year-old got straight As. The nine-year-old got all Es and Gs, and both of them made the honor roll, so I'm proud of them.

Now my thirteen-year-old says he wants to be a lawyer. He's really good at basketball, and people are looking at him for that already, but I tell him, "If you get hurt, what do you have to fall on? It's best that you keep going to school." He's decided he wants to go to college before he thinks about playing pro ball.

When I moved my kids to their new schools, I was looking for peace of mind that they would be safe and learning in a place where the teachers really care about the students. They have this at their schools now. These teachers want my boys to really advance in life. My sons loooooove going to school now. Ain't no more drama. My thirteen-year-old is in the process of feeling himself to be a man, so he doesn't say as much—although it's completely obvious how he feels when we have snow days, school's out, and he's complaining that he's missing classes—but the nine-year-old tells me stories about what the teachers have done with him and recites what he's learned. It's a huge difference from when he used to say that his teachers didn't like him. All of us were very blessed by getting these scholarships.

When children have different things to look forward to, they act differently. I just hope we can reach more people with this program and keep it going. You keep a program like this going, and you have people turning out a little different in society. You start to solve the bigger problems, too.

—Pamela, single mother of two

Beginning to Flourish

Rashawn's first-grade teacher gave him the worst grade you can give a child, yet he was reading and spelling well and counting above one hundred. His teacher said that the reason he got the poor grade was that he didn't raise his hand enough in class, so she had no way of telling how much he knew.

It's true: He was shy and didn't like crowds. He was reluctant to participate if there were too many people around or if the classroom behavior was chaotic. But I always thought that the teacher should have called on him rather than waiting for him to volunteer. I thought that was her job, to pull him out of his shell and encourage him to participate, to find out what he knew and what he needed. I also thought that if she could get the class under control, the children would have a better chance of learning.

When the school identified Rashawn as having a learning disability—in their words, he was "just a little behind"—the school counselor told me that if they could put him in special education, they could get him caught up.

Well, they didn't do it in six years.

Rashawn got labeled early on and then couldn't catch up after the school failed to help him get on course. I realize now he should never have been placed in a special-needs program. He should have received some extra attention in school, been challenged more, and he would have recovered from the minor setback. That was my mistake: accepting what they said.

By the time the scholarship fund tested him in the seventh grade, they found that he was two years behind. So that means that not only did the program he was in fail to bring him up to grade level, but while he was in it, he fell even farther behind.

Now, though, with the help of a scholarship to a private school where he is in a smaller class and the behavior problems of other students are nearly nonexistent, he's beginning to flourish. The first week after he started attending Bridge Academy, Rashawn came home, and my formerly shy and stand-offish boy excitedly said to me, "Pop, I'm making friends!"

Rashawn has a wonderful relationship with his teacher now. He's constantly telling me about Mr. Smith and what they're doing in school. His grades are coming up (he earned several As this year), his comprehension is improving, he's great in math, and I expect he'll be working on grade level in the next two years.

In the past, I was going to my children's schools two or three times a week to sort out some problem or to make sure my kids were okay. Now, the only time I'm at the school is when I'm volunteering in the classroom or meeting with teachers or administrators for a conference. I have peace of mind. I know they're safe. I know they're respected. I know they're learning.

—Joseph, single father and legal guardian

The Power of Choice

The minute my son received his preschool diploma, my mind started really thinking of his education from the beginning all the way to college. I had always wanted him to start at St. Thomas More Catholic School, and when he turned five, we started right there with some financial assistance from the archdiocese.

The school really helped him with discipline, self-respect, and reading. He attended St. Thomas More for kindergarten and first grade, but in 2000, I had to take him out because we couldn't afford to keep him there.

My son started attending a D.C. public school. Not long after, there was an incident on the school ground, and another parent and I had to go to court over a five-year-old who had brought a butter knife to school, but my son was blamed. I moved my son to another public school. I had thought that the teachers there would have recognized both his weaknesses and strengths in learning, but I was disappointed.

This school year, 2003–2004, he was accepted at a charter school, which I chose because of its similarities with private school. I am relieved to have him back in a better school.

In my family heritage, we've never had school choice before now—and now it's incredibly important. My son dreams of being a fireman when he graduates from high school, and I have another son with special needs. It's important to me that both of them have the opportunity to attend the schools that will work with their needs, give them the best education, and help them achieve their dreams. I am grateful that parental choice now exists in the District.

—Eva, mother of two

"A Hundred on My Spelling Test"

I got the twins two years ago because my brother was having problems. At first I registered them at Park View Elementary School, where I'd volunteered for years. Right away, Eric was having a lot of problems in the first grade, specifically with learning and paying attention, along with getting teased and picked on because he's a little fella. He wasn't progressing, so I had him tested for special education, and then he started attending special ed classes about sixteen hours a week. But he still didn't improve.

When the scholarship bill passed, I put in applications for both children, and they both received vouchers. I chose St. Gabriel's Catholic School because it's close to home and if the weather's bad, we can always walk to school. Besides, at Park View, the class size was about thirty kids, but at St. Gabriel's, it was down to about half that.

Eric started off still having a lot of problems, but then once he settled down and adjusted, he excelled tremendously! I could not believe how much his math, spelling, and reading improved. When he arrived at St. Gabriel's he couldn't spell many simple words, like "come" or "came" or the days of the week. But soon he was coming home and telling me, "Auntie, I got a hundred on my spelling test!"

Before, he really could not read, but now, he out-reads his sister. And sometimes Erica gets testy with him when he helps her with something: She'll say, "Go away! I could have figured that out myself!" I should say that Erica is doing really well, too. She was doing okay in public school, but in this new environment, she's improved tremendously. It's so nice to see both of them excel like this.

I pray and hope that with these scholarships, the public schools will have to come up to par, because right now we're losing too many of our young boys and girls to the streets. A lot of them give up on themselves. But with the scholarships, they can get the education that will give them better choices later on. With this help, they can go as far as they want to go. As long as they have the desire, they can climb and climb and climb.

—Catherine, legal guardian of two

You'll find additional parent stories in a wonderful book, *Trinnietta Gets a Chance: Six Families and Their School Choice Experience* by Daniel McGroarty. (Details are in appendix A, "Recommended Resources.") As you engage in your own campaign, stories like these will become familiar to you, as will the families who have lived them. Seek out inspirational accounts, encourage storytelling among your group, and share experiences with other leaders to help them keep up the fight, too.

8

Free at Last:
What Happens After You Win?

"Voucher Critics Vow to Fight on."
—*Headline from the Associated Press, published the day after passage of the D.C. School Choice Incentive Act of 2003, January 23, 2004*

When Congress authorized the voucher program for District families, I was having lunch with a supporter in Union Station, D.C.'s historic, bustling transportation hub. The upstairs features elegant restaurants, a food court and mall shops, while below ground, people are en route to all parts of the city. As I was talking with my lunch partner, who had just offered a generous donation to our organization, a staff member from Senator Bill Frist's (R-Tenn.) office rang my mobile phone to tell me the good news. I thanked him over and over again for the call, then hung up, told my companion that the legislation had passed, and both of us started jumping up and down, yelling our heads off, drawing stares and smiles from the business-suited diners around us.

The next day, I called all the parents together for a celebration of our own. Most of us whooped and hollered some more, some shook our heads in relieved disbelief, and others stood tall as we now knew our cause was affirmed by the nation's leaders. As we finished our time together, we held each other tight. For many, this felt like an ending, but I knew this was really the start of the most important phase of our effort. Aware of what was coming, I decided that this victory was a great reason to take the rest of the day off, my first in more than ten months.

The day after that, we got back to work.

We began the process of planning our outreach, figuring out how we could assist with the facilitation of the program, and we were full steam ahead once more.

To ensure that what you've fought for gets carried out fully and properly, and to defend against any further threats, there are five crucial steps to take after your legislation is passed:

1. *Take a break to recharge, but don't be gone too long.* If you disappear from the scene, you risk losing the credibility and relationships you've established. Instead, follow through and be a reminder that your organization is in this for the right reasons.

2. *Participate in the administration and outreach of the scholarship program.* Take a role in implementing and advocating the success of vouchers and voucher students in your area.

3. *Continue to serve and be visible in your community.* Keep the grassroots parent organization intact and use it to continue vital service to the community.

4. *Foster your relationships with lawmakers.* No doubt there will be additional legislative debate on this issue, if not right away, then certainly in the future. Maintain and strengthen your network among politicians.

5. *Prepare for legal attacks.* Most voucher programs are challenged in the courts. Be ready by staying on top of what's happening in other states and watching for threats in your own area.

Step 1. Take a break to recharge, but don't be gone too long.

One year, my neighbors and I worked with the city government to get a traffic light installed on a busy corner. When it went up, we were all happy to know our neighborhood would be safer, and then we went on with our lives. There was no need for follow-up phone calls or meetings. The job was done.

School choice advocacy is not like that.

After you win, you will be tempted to back off and rest. (I fantasized about the Bahamas and other warm island locales where I could lounge in my flip-flops. In fact, I still do.) It's difficult fighting for the legislation—so consuming that you may find yourself wishing you were finished just when the scholarship program is finally underway. Yet disappearing right after your legislation passes would be a terrible mistake. Not only is a whole new phase of work beginning for you, but this is an important time for helping the

> ### The Good Ol' Days?
>
> Making sure you stay strong for the parents after the win presents financial challenges, in that the grass roots get donations when they're trying to help pass legislation but money seems to evaporate when the fight's over. In some ways, it feels as if you're back at the beginning, pinching pennies and worrying about how to pay the electric bill. Yet if you follow the additional steps outlined in this chapter, and use what you've learned along the way, you can remain financially viable and responsible.

parents see that their trust in you was not misplaced: You always had in mind that the most important thing was to deliver vouchers to low-income families, and mere passage of law is only the first step, not the last.

When I talked recently with parents from Wisconsin and Ohio about what happened after their campaigns, they told me their organizations just faded out. Pilar and Roberta, two friends of mine who were leaders of the Cleveland and Milwaukee efforts more than a decade ago, told me that a year or so after their organizations closed their doors, their voucher programs were challenged and they had to reorganize. What a headache! Once a group loses momentum and cohesion, it's hard to re-create it. To this day, Milwaukee has difficulties with parents being organized.

Don't let this happen to you. Take the time you need to recuperate, assuming you've been putting in long hours and pretty much eating and sleeping for the movement. Do something entirely for yourself or your own family—then come back ready to tackle the next, all-important phase of parental choice: actually getting the vouchers into the hands of families who need them.

Step 2. Participate in the administration and outreach of the scholarship program.

No doubt an organization will be appointed to run your scholarship fund, and you should plan to participate in some capacity. Your role could be official or unofficial, encompassing anything from getting the word out on where and when scholarship applications will be available, to helping parents fill out forms, to working directly with the administrators to process paperwork, to advising parents about which schools will accept vouchers, and so on. D.C. Parents for School Choice has a contract with the Washington Scholarship Fund to make sure every corner of the city is being reached and that every parent who is eligible for the scholarship hears about it. We make sure the information gets deep into the community where qualified families live, and we help with application meetings in official partnership with the scholarship administrators.

Whether your organization takes on this level of responsibility or not, make sure you stay involved as the program is administered. What you don't want to do is spend a year advocating something and then vanish. I realize I'm repeating myself, but that's because this is so important: You have been the person to form relationships with parents, and it's essential that everyone knows you're still around. You've built a trust with them, and when the opposition comes out and repeats its false assertions and assumptions (see chapter 6 for a refresher on those), your continued presence in the program will keep parents assured that this is for real. I can't tell you how many parents contacted me, even after the program had been going for a while, to ask me if families really do receive vouchers or if this is some kind of shell game. Distrust of government-sponsored programs runs deep among minorities and people who are well below the poverty line. Be the bridge between those families and a better education for their children.

Step 3. Continue to serve and be visible in your community.

Why is it so common for low-income parents not to trust the government or advocacy groups? It's because they regularly hear promises and don't see a lot of action. Consider yourself an ambassador, someone who can be an inspiring exception to the rule.

To stay connected in the community, I still meet with the parent leadership once a month. As I mentioned, we work with the Washington Scholarship Fund, and we also participate in a project with the Department of Education to disseminate "No Child Left Behind" information. We continue to publish our newsletter and put out flyers to help parents with charter schools. We're staying in the game, still advocating for parental choice. We remain visible, attend education meetings, and are always sure to have representation at school board meetings. We still wear our T-shirts when we gather in public. We will keep ourselves in the community, not just for the scholarships, but for any issues that parents have to deal with in educating their children.

Part of your job will be to help people see that there's still vital work to be done, and to view their efforts as part of a larger whole across the nation. To connect you and your group to the bigger picture—which is the need for parental choice all across the U.S., specifically in urban centers with low-income populations—it's important to participate in organizations that are friendly to school choice. By joining, you can hear stories and learn from other people's successes and failures, plus you can meet other parent organizers and support one another. (You'll find a number of organizations listed in appendix C.) One of my favorites is the Black Alliance for Educational Options, because attending their events always revitalizes me. It's inspiring to be around hundreds of people who believe in the same thing you do, and it can reenergize you and help you stay committed. Dr. Howard Fuller, who wrote the foreword to this book, has always been particularly inspirational to me. He makes me and many others want to get out there and fight another day to get children the best education we can.

Be aware that your group will need additional support from you. Specifically, many parents who've been active in the campaign will need your help to make a difficult transition. Democracy can be heady stuff, and reaching a big goal can sometimes feel like more of a letdown than an achievement. This was certainly something we had to contend with in D.C., where parents had not only been interacting with famous politicians, both local and national, but also in some cases appearing on TV or being quoted in the newspaper.

Aside from the media attention, participating in a campaign like this can and should give parents an incredible boost in self-worth. One woman once came to me with tears in her eyes, and said, "This is the most important thing I've ever done." She had gotten pregnant as a teenager, her family had ostracized her ever since, and they'd always maintained that she would never amount to anything. During the campaign, she was so involved, and it made her feel so good about herself. I especially remember when she appeared on TV and handled herself very well, and her mother said to her, probably for the first time ever, that she was proud of her daughter.

For someone who has spent a lifetime trying to prove something, and she is finally validated, what's next once the goal has been attained?

It reminds me of something I once read about the first astronauts to land on the moon: After they'd made that flight, most of them suffered a period of some degree of depression. After all, what do you do after you've been to the moon? What in the future can possibly top or even match that?

Let parents know you'll be there for them as they deal with the comedown after the conclusion of the legislative campaign. Sometimes, parents complain, "You don't call me anymore!" It's important to handle this delicately and be sensitive to their feelings. You'll be working with people every day for many months, and all of a sudden, you won't be with them so often, and feelings are bound to get hurt.

One parent said to me, "I feel used." It was actually the same woman I mentioned just a few paragraphs ago, who had felt that the campaign was the most important thing she'd ever done.

I just had to empathize and help her understand: "You know, sometimes I feel that way, too. But we were on the right side of history, that's for sure. It's okay to feel what you feel, but it's also important to remember why we all did this: for our children and grandchildren."

Occasionally, I find myself reminding parents that playing the victim in the middle of such an exciting victory underplays their own power. This campaign was not about me or my personal agenda. Yes, I got things started. I began this as one mother fighting for her child, and it became thousands of parents fighting for their children. I did the best I could for them and by them, but I didn't force anyone, or even beg anyone, to come along. I provided the means and the opportunity, but ultimately everyone made their own decisions. It's important for parents to own that, to realize how incredibly powerful they've been, and to keep from minimizing or disrespecting their own contribution.

Step 4. Foster your relationships with lawmakers.

In our case, Congress authorized vouchers as a five-year pilot program with the money appropriated annually. This means that, in 2008, vouchers in the District will be up for a vote again. So we're learning now who will be supportive of this new legislation and nurturing relationships with them.

In addition, as the funding comes up for approval each year, we want our views considered and hope to influence this key decision, so we need to stay in touch with the legislators. We make sure that Congress knows how the program is going from our perspective. As a result, anytime vouchers are in the news, someone from Congress calls me to find out what I think about it, and I'm able to pass on the parents' viewpoints.

Ongoing relationships with members of both the House and the Senate are vital. Frequently, I touch base with several Congressmen, particularly the co-authors of the legislation, Representatives Boehner and Davis. I still meet with their staffs regularly to see if there's anything I can do for them, to see if there's anything they need to know, or to talk about anything they've heard. They invite me to participate in formal meetings, as well.

You can anticipate the same kind of needs arising as a voucher program gets implemented in your area, too. Regardless of whether your state includes a renewal clause or not, here's what you can do:

- ✓ Expect to nurture the relationships you have by offering support and opinions, keeping politicians connected with the grass roots.
- ✓ Meet any new/incoming legislators, and see who will be on your side the next time you fight.

✓ Make yourself available for meetings and joint media appearances.

Step 5. Prepare for legal attacks.

Although vouchers have been upheld in the courts most of the times they've been challenged, opponents continue to bring cases against them. The best thing you can do is to have your troops ready by following the preceding four steps; this puts you in position to close ranks quickly when the need arises.

Indeed, staying involved in your community makes sure you'll be there when the opposition attacks, or when it's time for renewals, or when it's time to fight for something new to do with the legislation. Just know that the legal challenges will come. Not long before I wrote this chapter, Colorado lost their court battle with the National Education Association and the People for the American Way in the state supreme court. (The Colorado Supreme Court ruled against the program on a Colorado-specific law regarding local control of schools.) Florida is fighting a court case right now, and Arizona recently won a challenge to the tax-credit program.

Anytime a program fails to serve the right kids, somebody behaves fraudulently, or there's some other impropriety—or perceived impropriety—a voucher program opens itself up to a lawsuit. (All the more reason for your parents' group to stay active, right? You can help your administrators walk the straight and narrow.) In some states, lawsuits have a great deal less to do with the actual program than with the opposition's financial and political strength.[§]

While we were celebrating our victory at our parents' luncheon the day after Congress approved our legislation, newspapers were printing the headline, "Voucher Critics Vow to

---

[§] There are organizations to help you if and when you are faced with legal challenges. One is the Institute for Justice, which I've mentioned a few times in the book and included in appendix C.

Fight On," so I certainly don't think D.C. is exempt. Our program is strong now, but it got off to a rocky start, and it's very possible that the mistakes made early on will come back to haunt us in the future. The opposition is bound to use the first year against us. And if it ever goes to court . . . who knows?

We do know that opportunity scholarships are making an important difference for many families in the District, and we know it's due in large part to the courage, heart, and dedication of D.C. parents.

What's more, we know that whenever anyone wants to hear about what happened, to challenge our position, or to assist us in our ongoing efforts, we're ready to give our side of the story, to activate the parents and call on them to sound their voices again.

My final words of advice: *Stay organized.* Don't let your group fall apart. And if there's ever anything I can do to assist you, don't hesitate to call on me. Send me an e-mail, write to me, call me. Let's get together and learn from one another. I'd be delighted to address your organization or help you in some capacity. Know that I'm here for you, and for the parents who desire and deserve more for their children.

About the Author

Virginia Walden Ford is executive director of D.C. Parents for School Choice, a grassroots organization of the District's parents. The group was crucial to the passage of the "three-sector bill" in 2004, which provided private scholarships to low-income parents, as well as funding to public and charter schools in Washington, D.C.

Mrs. Ford is the daughter of educators. Her father was the first African-American administrator in the Little Rock school district, and her mother was one of the first black teachers in a previously all-white school.

Mrs. Ford graduated from Central High, the same school the Little Rock Nine had attended just a few years before. Later, as a single mom in Washington, D.C., she became an education advocate, working to get the word out on the District's charter schools. At the same time, her own son was one of the casualties of D.C. public schools, which were ranked among the worst in the nation. He was failing classes and hanging out with a bad crowd when a private scholarship helped him turn his life around. This fortified her commitment to school choice, and when it became clear that parents would need to organize if they wanted to make vouchers a reality, she took the bull by the horns.

Regarded as a dedicated, persistent, gracious leader in the school choice movement, Mrs. Ford continues to work in our nation's capital to ensure that opportunity scholarships remain an option for D.C. parents.

Contact her by sending your e-mail message to wdcparentschoice@aol.com, or call the D.C. Parents for School Choice office at (202) 546-4304.

Appendix A
Recommended Resources

An Education Agenda
Let Parents Choose Their Children's School
John C. Goodman and Fritz E. Steiger, eds.
National Center for Policy Analysis (2001)

> To order, contact NCPA's Publication Department at (972) 386-6272 or ncpa@ncpa.org, or mail your request to NCPA, 12770 Coit Rd., #800, Dallas, TX 75251 ($10 ea., discounts for bulk)

> From the NCPA's website, NCPA.org: . . . an excellent resource for anyone seeking a broad overview of school choice from some of its most articulate advocates. In an effort to help Congress and the Bush Administration encourage reform of the nation's public schools, the NCPA and Children First America published [this] book of essays from the nation's leading education experts, including Nobel Prize–winning economist Milton Friedman.

Angry Parents, Failing Schools
What's Wrong with the Public Schools and What You Can Do About It
Elaine K. McEwan
Harold Shaw Publishers (2000)

> From a review on MathematicallyCorrect.com (http://www.mathematicallycorrect.com/mcewan.htm): . . . a valuable source book for parents who are concerned about the education of their children.

> Elaine McEwan paints a sad but realistic picture . . . includes sections devoted to understanding the jargon of the educrats—the new meanings for old words and other phrases used to disguise much of the problem and how to interpret what they really mean. Throughout, readers will also find helpful advice and resources

they can use as they confront this problem in their own lives, in their own schools, and for their own children.

Building the Base
A Blueprint for Grassroots Leaders in the School Choice Movement
Donna Watson et al.
Children First America (2003)
Available by contacting D.C. Parents for School Choice at
(202) 546-4304 ($30 ea.)

This training manual was developed in response to the many scholarship program directors, parent organizers, and community/religious leaders around the country who needed technical support on how to organize the grass roots on the school choice issue. This how-to guide is designed to help motivate, educate, and activate parents and others in the community to work toward public policy change.

Not Yet "Free at Last"
The Unfinished Business of the Civil Rights Movement
Our Battle for School Choice
Mikel Holt
Institute for Contemporary Studies (1999)

From a description in *Issues & Views* **(Summer/Fall 1999):** In Mikel Holt's blow-by-blow description of the battle against the education establishment in Milwaukee, we get to meet the people and learn of the events that led to the city's pioneering school voucher program. His book . . . exposes the bureaucratic corruption and intense media bias that often seemed impossible to surmount. Holt refers to the victory over these forces as a ride on a "new Freedom Train."

Organizing
A Guide for Grassroots Leaders
Si Kahn
National Association of Social Workers (NASW) Press (1991)

From a description on Amazon.com: . . . [A] dynamic guide on how to unite people for change, to help people work together to get things done. It describes how to influence power structures, how to become successful organizers and fundraisers, and how to effect social change through grassroots organization and mobilization. Special Features: emphasizes practicality versus theory, presents step-by-step guidelines for change, provides a framework for multiracial organizing.

Trinnietta Gets a Chance
Six Families and Their School Choice Experience
Daniel McGroarty
The Heritage Foundation (2001)

From a description on Amazon.com: Featuring the stories of six inner-city families struggling to provide quality education for their children, [this book] makes a powerful case for parental involvement and school choice. It also vividly shows the obstacles these families face and the joy they experience when their children flourish thanks to competition in education.

Voucher Wars
Waging the Legal Battle Over School Choice
Clint Bolick
Cato Institute (2003)

From a review by Jonathan Butcher in Townhall.com http://www.townhall.com/bookclub/bolick.html): . . . the definitive history of school choice litigation. The book traces [the Institute for Justice's] progress within the movement from the first arguments in a sweltering Milwaukee courtroom to the strategy meeting held in the "Shadow of the Beast" to the "Super Bowl for school choice" in Cleveland. Legal arguments have been pivotal to the movement because opponents have challenged every school choice program. IJ has been at the lead in school choice cases around the U.S., including those in Milwaukee, Ohio, Florida, Maine, Arizona, Vermont, and Puerto Rico. The firm's efforts have not only provided the movement with crucial legal victories but have also enabled students to continue to participate in choice programs while court battles raged.

Appendix B
Key Studies to Support School Choice

School Choice: Doing It the Right Way Makes a Difference
http://www.schoolchoiceinfo.org/data/research/20031116schoolchoicereport.pdf
> The National Working Commission on Choice in K–12 Education
> The Brookings Institution (November 2003)
> 46 pages

Milwaukee's Public Schools in an Era of Choice
http://www.schoolchoiceinfo.org/data/research/ACF6pnkza.pdf
> American Education Reform Council (October 2003)
> 4 pages

When Schools Compete: The Effects on Florida Public School Achievement
http://www.schoolchoiceinfo.org/data/research/Voucher_Effect_on_Fla._schools
> Jay P. Greene and Marcus A. Winters
> The Manhattan Institute for Policy Research (August 2003)
> 24 pages

Vouchers for Special Education Students
An Evaluation of Florida's McKay Scholarship Program
http://www.schoolchoiceinfo.org/data/research/Greene_McKay.pdf
> Jay P. Greene
> The Manhattan Institute for Policy Research (June 2003)
> 39 pages

Schools that Choice Built
http://www.schoolchoiceinfo.org/data/research/SchoolsBuilt.pdf
> Abigail Winger
> American Education Reform Council (January 2003)
> 4 pages

Rising to the Challenge
The Effect of School Choice on Public Schools in Milwaukee and San Antonio
http://www.schoolchoiceinfo.org/data/research/GreenePS2.pdf

Jay P. Greene

The Manhattan Institute for Policy Research (October 2002)

12 pages

Appendix C
Friends of School Choice (Organizations)

The Alliance for School Choice

AllianceforSchoolChoice.org

> Clint Bolick, President and General Counsel
> 5080 N. 40th St., Suite 375
> Phoenix, AZ 85018
> Phone: (602) 468-0900
> Fax: (602) 468-0920
> E-mail: info@allianceforschoolchoice.org

The Alliance is a national nonprofit educational policy group advocating school choice programs across the country. A reorganization of three smaller education reform groups (American Education Reform Council, American Education Reform Foundation, and Children First America), the Alliance provides leadership, experience, and resources to affect meaningful reform in the educational arena. It's mission is to improve our nation's system of K–12 education by advancing public policy that empowers parents, particularly in low-income families, to choose the education they determine is best for their children.

American Education Reform Council and Foundation

SchoolChoiceInfo.org

> Susan Mitchell, President
> 2025 North Summit Ave., Suite 103
> Milwaukee, WI 53202
> Phone: (414) 319-9160
> Fax: (414) 765-0220
> E-mail: Mitchell@parentchoice.org

The American Education Reform Council, or AERC, is a nonprofit organization based in Milwaukee that provides information about the impact of parental choice. Its companion foundation, the AERF, assists supporters across the country in expanding publicly financed parental choice options.

American Legislative Exchange Council
Alec.org

Duane Parde, Executive Director
1129 20th St., NW, Suite 500
Washington, DC 20036
Phone: (202) 466-3800
Fax: (202) 466-3801
E-mail: info@alec.org

More than a quarter century ago, a small group of legislators and conservative policy advocates met in Chicago to implement a vision that continues in this organization today. It is a bipartisan membership association for conservative state lawmakers who share a common belief in limited government, free markets, federalism, and individual liberty.

Association of Christian Schools International
ACSI.org

Ken Smitherman, President
P.O. Box 65130
Colorado Springs, CO 80962
Phone: (719) 528-6906 & (800) 367-0798
Fax: (719) 531-0631
E-mail: urbanservices@acsi.org

The Association of Christian Schools International, or ACSI, was founded in 1978. In addition to its headquarters facility in Colorado Springs, ACSI has sixteen regional offices in North America and around the globe. Current membership includes 5,000 member schools from 115 countries with an enrollment of 1,030,000 students. Programs and services are designed to assist Christian schools at every grade level, including early education and higher education.

Black Alliance for Educational Options
BAEO.org

> Lawrence Patrick, III, President and CEO
> 1710 Rhode Island Ave., NW, Suite 1200
> Washington, DC 20036
> Phone: (202) 429-2236
> Fax: (202) 429-2237

The Black Alliance for Educational Options, or BAEO, is a national, nonpartisan member organization whose mission is to actively support parental choice to empower families and increase educational options for black children. Dr. Howard Fuller, BAEO Chairman, launched the organization in August 2000; local chapters around the nation have been and are currently being formed.

Center for Educational Freedom (Cato Institute)
Cato.org

> David F. Salisbury, Director
> 1000 Massachusetts Ave., NW
> Washington, DC 20001
> Phone: (202) 842-0200
> Fax: (202) 842-3490
> E-mail: dsalisbury@cato.org

As center director, Dr. David F. Salisbury explores and promotes education reform policies and private initiatives that will strengthen the independent education system. The Cato Institute, founded in 1977, seeks to broaden the parameters of public policy debate to allow consideration of the traditional American principles of limited government, individual liberty, free markets, and peace. Toward that goal, the Institute strives to achieve greater involvement of the intelligent, concerned lay public in questions of policy and the proper role of government.

Center for Education Reform

EdReform.com

> Jeanne Allen, President
> 1001 Connecticut Ave., NW, Suite 204
> Washington, DC 20036
> Phone: (202) 822-9000 & 800-521-2118
> Fax: (202) 822-5077
> E-mail: cer@edreform.com

The Center for Education Reform opened its doors in 1993 to assist parents all over America in choosing the best possible education for their children. They knew that parents often lacked the information they needed, so CER set out to educate, inform, and empower parents and to transform schools caught in the one-size-fits-all trap. Inspired by the old maxim, "knowledge is power," CER publishes a newsletter titled *Parent Power!* (http://www.edreform.com/parentpower) for parents who want to know more about the issues that affect their children's education.

Children's Scholarship Fund

ScholarshipFund.org

> Darla Romfo, President and COO
> 8 West 38th St., 9th Floor
> New York, NY 10018-6229
> Phone: (212) 515-7100
> Fax: (212) 515-7111
> E-mail: info@scholarshipfund.org

In 1998, the Children's Scholarship Fund was created to provide parents, children, and teachers with new ways of thinking about how we fund and deliver education in the United States. Low-income parents of more than 1.25 million children applied for scholarships, demonstrating an overwhelming demand for an alternative to the nation's government schools.

Clare Booth Luce Policy Institute

CBLPolicyInstitute.org

Michelle Easton, President
112 Elden St., Suite P
Herndon, VA 20170
Phone: (703) 318-0730
Fax: (703) 318-8867
E-mail: cblpi@erols.com

The Clare Booth Luce Policy Institute's dual missions are to prepare young women for effective conservative leadership and to promote school choice opportunities for all K–12 children in America. Through their national Conservative Women Speakers Program, seminars and conferences, mentoring sessions, Web site, quarterly newsletter, policy issue papers, and an aggressive media campaign, they give young women hands-on training in countering radical feminism and fighting for conservative principles.

D.C. Parents for School Choice

DCParentsforSchoolChoice.com

Virginia Walden Ford, Executive Director
809 Virginia Ave., SE
Washington, DC 20003
Phone: (202) 546-4304
E-mail: wdcparentschoice@aol.com

Founded in 1998 after President Clinton vetoed the D.C. Student Opportunity Scholarship Act, D.C. Parents for School Choice trains and empowers parents in the District of Columbia on how to make informed educational decisions for their children. Its Parent Resource Center provides information on public charter schools, traditional public schools, private schools, scholarship programs, after-school and summer enrichment programs, tutorials, and other programs that offer enrichment to students.

Education Leaders Council
EducationLeaders.org
> Theodore Rebarber, Chief Executive Officer
> 1225 19th St., Suite 240
> Washington, DC 20036
> Phone: (202) 261-2600
> Fax: (202) 261-2619
> E-mail: info@educationleaders.org

Begun in 1995, ELC is an organization that represents leaders in education—state department leaders, school board members, administrators, etc.—who are committed to the kinds of fundamental reforms demanded by millions of parents yet often ignored by national organizations. Its belief is that the focus of education should be on students, not the school system.

Excellent Education for Everyone (E3)
NJE3.org
> Dan Gaby, Executive Director
> 45 Academy St., Suite 501
> Newark, NJ 07102
> Phone: (973) 273-7217
> Fax: (973) 273-7222

E3 is a nonprofit organization devoted to educating New Jersey residents about how parental school choice can improve urban public schools. E3 believes that equal opportunity to a good education is a fundamental civil right that is being denied to our most needy children.

Fight for Children
FightforChildren.org
> Kaleem Caire, Executive Director
> 1825 K Street, NW
> Suite 1080
> Washington, DC 20006

Phone: (202) 772-0400
Fax: (202) 772-0401

Fight for Children creates, promotes, and invests in K–12 education opportunities that successfully prepare children for college and the workplace, and provides quality primary health care options for our youth.

Florida Education Freedom Foundation
FloridaPride.org (link to FEFF)
Denise Lasher, President
601 North Ashley Dr., Suite 300
Tampa, FL 33602
Phone: (813) 318-0995
Fax: (813) 318-0556
E-mail: dlasher@feff.org

Florida Education Freedom Foundation serves as a resource organization and clearinghouse for Florida's scholarship funding organizations (SFOs). FEFF works in concert with the SFOs to strengthen and expand the corporate income tax credit scholarship.

Greater Educational Opportunities (GEO) Foundation
GEOFoundation.org
Kevin Teasley, President and CEO
302 South Meridian St., Suite 201
Indianapolis, IN 46225
Phone: (317) 524-3770
Fax: (317) 524-3773
E-mail: teasleygeo@aol.com

GEO Foundation believes that all children should have access to a quality education. It embraces many educational options that enable parents to help their children learn and schools to succeed. Through an aggressive community outreach and the introduction of options that empower families, the GEO Foundation strives to make educational choice a reality for all children.

Heartland Institute
Heartland.org
> Joe Bast, President
> 19 South LaSalle, Suite 903
> Chicago, IL 60603
> Phone: (312) 377-4000
> Fax: (312) 377-5000
> E-mail: think@heartland.org

The mission of the Heartland Institute is to help build social movements in support of ideas that empower people. Such ideas include parental choice in education, market-based approaches to environmental protection, privatization of public services, and deregulation in areas where property rights and markets do a better job than government bureaucracies. *School Reform News* is published monthly by the Heartland Institute.

Heritage Foundation
Heritage.org
> Edwin J. Feulner, Jr., President
> 214 Massachusetts Ave., NE
> Washington, DC 20002-4999
> Phone: (202) 546-4400
> Fax: (202) 546-8328

Founded in 1973, the Heritage Foundation is a research and educational institute, a think tank whose mission is to formulate and promote conservative public policies based on the principles of free enterprise, limited government, individual freedom, traditional American values, and a strong national defense. Education reform is a key issue of the Heritage Foundation, and they publish *School Choice: What's Happening in the States* annually.

Hispanic Council for Reform and Educational Options
HCREO.org

Rebeca Nieves-Huffman, President
2600 Virginia Ave., NW, Suite 408
Washington, DC 20037
Phone: (202) 625-6766 & (877) 888-2736
Fax: (202) 625-6767
E-mail: rhuffman@hcreo.org

The Hispanic CREO's mission is to improve educational outcomes for Hispanic children by empowering families through parental choice in education. This newly formed organization's purpose is to be a national voice for the right of Hispanic families to access all educational options and to be an agent for equity and quality in education.

Institute for Justice
IJ.org

William "Chip" Mellor, President
1717 Pennsylvania Ave., NW, Suite 200
Washington, DC 20006
Phone: (202) 955-1300
Fax: (202) 955-1329
E-mail: general@ij.org

The Institute for Justice is a libertarian public interest law firm founded in 1991. It litigates to secure economic liberty, school choice, private property rights, freedom of speech, and other vital individual liberties, and to restore constitutional limits on the power of government. In addition, it trains law students, lawyers, and policy activists in the tactics of public interest litigation to advance individual rights. Through these activities, the Institute challenges the ideology of the welfare state and illustrates and extends the benefits of freedom to those whose full enjoyment of liberty is denied by government.

Milton and Rose D. Friedman Foundation

FriedmanFoundation.org

Gordon St. Angelo, President and CEO

One American Sq., Suite 2420

P.O. Box 82078

Indianapolis, IN 46282

Phone: (317) 681-0745

Fax: (317) 681-0945

The mission of the Friedman Foundation is to promote public understanding of the need for major reform in K–12 education and of the role that competition through educational choice can play in achieving that reform.

REACH Alliance (the Road to Educational Achievement through Choice)

PASchoolchoice.org

Andrew LeFevre, Executive Director

P.O. Box 1283

Harrisburg, PA 17108

Phone: (717) 238-1878

Fax: (717) 703-3182

E-mail: alefevre@paschoolchoice.org

In 1991, the grassroots coalition of REACH Alliance was founded to coordinate efforts to pass school choice legislation in Pennsylvania. Since then, REACH Alliance has grown into a broad, diverse coalition that includes members from the business community, labor unions, ethnic and religious organizations, parents, and taxpayer groups.

State Policy Network

SPN.org

Tracie Sharp, President

6255 Arlington Blvd.

Richmond, CA 94805-1601

Phone: (510) 965-9700
Fax: (510) 965-9701
E-mail: spn@spn.org

State Policy Network (SPN) is the professional service
organization for America's state-based, free market, think tank
movement. Founded in 1992, SPN is the only group in the country
dedicated solely to improving the practical effectiveness of
independent, nonprofit, market-oriented, state-based think tanks. State
Policy Network's programs enable these organizations to better
educate local citizens, policymakers, and opinion leaders about market-
oriented alternatives to state and local policy challenges. A
membership directory is available on the SPN website, and school
choice supporters can access SPN member organizations located in
their individual states.

Thomas B. Fordham Foundation
EdExcellence.net
Chester E. Finn, Jr., President
1627 K St., NW, Suite 600
Washington, DC 20006
Phone: (202) 223-5452
Fax: (202) 223-9226
E-mail: backtalk@edexcellence.net

The Thomas B. Fordham Foundation supports research,
publications, and action projects of national significance in
elementary/secondary education reform, as well as significant
education reform projects in Dayton, Ohio, and vicinity. It has
assumed the work of the Educational Excellence Network and is
affiliated with the Manhattan Institute for Policy Research, which
publishes the Education Freedom Index of the States. Fordham is
the publisher of the *Education Gadfly*, a weekly bulletin of news
and analysis.

United States Department of Education
Ed.gov

> Margaret Spellings, Secretary of Education
> 400 Maryland Ave., SW
> Washington, DC 20202-0100
> Phone: (202) 401-2000
> E-mail: usalearn@ed.gov

With the inauguration of President George W. Bush in 2001, the U.S. Department of Education was transformed into a school choice–supportive and parent-friendly governmental agency.

General Information:
Toll Free: (800) USA-LEARN (800-872-5327)
Se Habla Español TTY: (800) 437-0833

This telephone number is for information on the Department of Education's major education improvement priorities (e.g., reading, family involvement, technology). Services provided by the Information Resource Center include information on the Department's programs and agenda, registration for satellite events, and directory assistance for the Department, as well as referrals to Department specialists or other experts.

No Child Left Behind (**NCLB.gov**):
If you have comments or questions about the No Child Left Behind law or its programs, call (888) 814-NCLB (888-814-6252) or TTY (800) 437-0833. Send e-mail to nochildleftbehind@ed.gov.

Appendix D
D.C. School Choice Campaign Timeline

1980s   The school choice movement begins.[1]

1998   **D.C. Parents for School Choice** is founded to help charter school parents understand the first eighteen charter schools starting in D.C. The clearinghouse was funded by the Bradley Foundation in Milwaukee and Children First America (led by John Walton). In time, the organization expands its outreach to serve all parents in all schools as they try to help their children get the best education possible.

President Clinton vetoes a bill to give two thousand low-income D.C. parents up to $3,200 a year per child to send students to the parents' school of choice.[2]

Virginia Walden writes an editorial in the *Washington Post* titled "Vouchers Deserved a Chance" in response to Clinton's veto of the school choice bill championed by Senator Joseph Lieberman (D-Conn.).[3]

National Catholic Register reports that D.C. seems a logical place to institute school choice (per-pupil spending is among the highest in the nation, yet standardized test scores are below national averages; dropout rates are high; and deteriorating facilities often result in lengthy school closings). There is no

---

[1] Hickey, Jennifer G. "Washington Diary: Reforming the Education Debate," *Insight on the News,* July 21, 2003.
< http://www.insightmag.co.../Washington.Diaryreforming.The.Education. Debate-447800.shtm >
[2] Walden, Virginia. "Vouchers Deserved a Chance," *Washington Post:* May 24, 1998.
[3] Walden. Ibid.

political support for school choice programs among the mayoral candidates, however.[4]

The U.S. Supreme Court upholds the constitutionality of Wisconsin's Milwaukee Parental Choice Program by a vote of eight to one. The suit was brought by the ACLU, People for the American Way, and the NAACP. The Landmark Legal Foundation defended the program in court and called the outcome a "watershed victory for education reformers across the nation."[5]

Having seen Walden's editorial in the *Washington Post* (see above), former senator Larry Pressler (R-S.D.) contacts her to suggest she run for mayor of D.C. with his backing. When she declines, he considers running himself.[6]

2000 **A study of 810 students,** co-authored by Paul E. Peterson (director of the Program on Education Policy and Governance at Harvard University), concludes that African-American elementary students in D.C. who transferred to private schools with the help of vouchers were happier with the new school and did better in math than their peers. Middle and junior high students did not fare as well. Private-school students' parents were more satisfied with teacher-parent relations and with teacher skills than in the public schools. All students found discipline at the private schools stricter.[7]

---

[4] Murray, William. "School Choice Looks for a Political Champion in Washington," *National Catholic Register:* October 11, 1998.
[5] Thomas, Cal. "School Choice Scores a Victory," *Washington Times:* November 15, 1998.
[6] Powell, Michael. "Ex-Senator for Mayor?" *Washington Post:* June 12, 1998.
[7] Mathews, Jay. "Vouchers Earn Positive Marks: Elementary School Students Show Success, Study Finds," *Washington Post,* February 28, 2000.

> *"Vouchers are a tax break for parents who already*
> *have children in private schools."*
> –Representative Jesse Jackson, Jr. (D-Ill.)[8]

> *"This is the first time I've seen a way for black kids*
> *to get out of bad schools."* –Virginia Walden Ford[9]

2001   **On April 12,** Walden Ford visits President George W. Bush at his invitation, along with Dr. Tina Dupree of Florida Child, and students and parents led by Children First America.[10]

On April 16, Walden Ford testifies before the Committee on Education and the Workforce.[11]

Walden Ford writes an editorial in the *Washington Post* titled "Still Separate and Unequal," urging politicians and voters to "close the racial gap" and "promote desegregation" that exists in the "two school systems" in D.C.: "one for the rich, and the other for the rest of us."[12]

2002   **The "No Child Left Behind" law,** signed by President Bush, offers public school choice to students in failing schools and authorizes the use of Title I dollars for tutoring and supplemental services.

On February 20, Walden Ford calls for parents to rally around the cause of school choice on the Supreme Court Steps, as the constitutionality of vouchers is again before the court.[13]

---

[8] McQueen, Anjetta. "School Vouchers Urged for Minorities," *SpeakOut.com*, August 24, 2000. < http://speakout.com/activism/apstories/1656-1.html >
[9] Ibid.
[10] "D.C.'s Virginia Walden Ford, Florida's Dr. Tina Dupree Captivate the President," *Children First America*, June 2001.
[11] Testimony of Virginia Walden Ford, April 16, 2001. < http://edworkforce.house.gov/hearings/107th/fc/edtax41602/ford.htm >
[12] Walden Ford, Virginia. "Still Separate and Unequal," *Washington Post*, October 21, 2001.
[13] Walden Ford, Virginia. "It's Time to Rally Around the Cause," *Alternatives*, February 2002.

In *Zelman v. Doris Simmons-Harris*, the ruling affirms the constitutionality of the Cleveland voucher program. President Bush calls it "a landmark ruling."[14]

The National PTA's Legislation Committee Chair, Latha Krishnaiyer, testifies against vouchers and tuition tax credits before the House Committee on Education and the Workforce.[15]

The Washington Teachers Union is found to have misspent $4.6 million of the union's treasury monies to fund their lavish lifestyles. The damage to the organization's political clout just as the voucher debate heats up is serious.[16]

D.C. Mayor Anthony Williams begins talks with school choice supporters close to White House and congressional leaders and soon becomes an ally of the cause.[17]

2003   **In February, Representative Jeff Flake** (R-Ariz.) introduces his school choice bill.[18] A press conference, including D.C. parents, is held.

In March, D.C. Councilman Kevin Chavous calls a town hall meeting to discuss school choice. D.C. Parents for School Choice brings most of the 113 parents who attend, and 21 speak in support of school choice.

---

[14] Weyrich, Paul M. "Notable News Now—School Choice: Give the Public Schools Some Needed Competition," *FreeCongress.org*, October 24, 2002. < http://www.freecongress.org/commentaries/2002/021024PW.asp >
[15] "This Week in Washington," *PTA.org*, April 19, 2002. < http://www.pta.org/ptawashington/news/dcnews/020419.asp
[16] Hsu, Spencer S. "How Vouchers Came to D.C.," *Education Next*, Fall 2004. < http://www.educationnext.org/20044/44.html >
[17] Hsu, "How Vouchers ..." Ibid.
[18] Gannon, Jeff. "House Approves D.C. School Vouchers; Challenge in Senate Expected," *Talon News*, September 9, 2003. < http://www.talonnews.com/news/2003/september/0909_vouchers_house. shtml >

In April, Representatives Tom Davis (R-Va.) and John Boehner (R-Ohio) introduce their own school choice bill, which ultimately passes in the House in September 2003. (Flake withdraws his own bill and supports Davis-Boehner.)

In May, D.C. Mayor Anthony Williams endorses vouchers and gets lambasted by D.C. Representative Eleanor Holmes Norton. He's also accused of being a "closet Republican" and a traitor to his (black) race.[19]

In July, President Bush addresses Kipp D.C. Academy and guests regarding education reform and parental options. He praises the D.C. charter school program and announces he's going to request $75 million from Congress for a choice incentive fund.[20]

Two senators, Arlen Specter (R-Pa.) and Mary Landrieu (D-La.), reverse their positions on school choice, shocking and angering voucher supporters. In the hall after the Appropriations Committee vote, nine-year-old Mosiyah Hall, a public school student, asks Landrieu where she sends her own children to school. The senator tells him that her children go to Georgetown Day, a private school in D.C. She also tells the assembled parents that vouchers wouldn't help them, because Georgetown Day is too expensive and they still wouldn't be able to afford it. Many feel insulted by her comment.[21]

---

[19] "A Mayor Breakthrough: D.C. Democrats Back Education Vouchers," *WSJ.com,* May 11, 2003.
< http://www.opionionjounral.com/editorial/feature.html?id=110003480 >
[20] Bush, George W. "President Discusses Education Reform in DC," *USInfo.state.gov,* July 1, 2003.
< http://usinfo.state.gov/usa/edu/s0701013.htm >
[21] McGurn, William. "Betraying D.C.'s Children: Where do your kids go to school, Mary Landrieu?" *WSJ.com,* July 24, 2003.
< http://www.opionionjournal.com/editorial/feature.html?id-110003789 >

Senator Dianne Feinstein (D-Calif.) backs vouchers in D.C.: "Local leaders should have the opportunity to experiment with programs that they believe are right for their area. This is the case in San Francisco. This is the case in Wichita. And I believe it should be the case in the District as well . . ."[22]

"There is no consistent evidence that private school tuition vouchers improve educational opportunities for students in private or public schools."
–Reg Weaver, head of the National Education Association[23]

"He's wrong in his implication about the money, and he's wrong in his description of the research. There's disagreement out there, and the evidence is not absolutely definitive. But if we held any other education policy up to the standard he appears to be requiring of vouchers, we wouldn't be doing anything in schools because there wouldn't be evidence to support anything."
– Jay P. Greene, a senior fellow at the conservative Manhattan Institute for Policy Research[24]

"We can't keep telling parents to wait. We have to provide choices right now. I'm very hopeful that the school system will improve itself. Interestingly enough, they're talking about all of this in light of the fact that parents are looking for other options. This is something that should have been done a long time ago."
–Virginia Walden Ford[25]

---

[22] "Dianne Feinstein Backs Vouchers," *Vermonters for Better Education,* July 28, 2003. < http://www.schoolreport.com/vbe/nlet/07_28_03.htm >
[23] Bluey, Robert B. "Union: Higher Teacher Pay, Not Vouchers, Results in Better Education," *The Daily News,* July 9, 2003.
< http://www.childrenfirstamerica.org/DailyNews/03Jul/0709035.htm >
[24] Ibid.
[25] Ibid.

The National Education Association campaigns against vouchers during the August congressional recess.[26]

The Bush administration backs a $17 million school choice plan for the District. It is supported by a number of Democrats and cosponsored by both Republicans and Democrats. The plan is to provide scholarship vouchers of up to $7,500 by lottery to about 2,000 families who want to move their children to private schools.[27]

After Senator Ted Kennedy (D-Mass.) promises to filibuster to obstruct a school voucher bill, Walden Ford appears in an ad, asking him how he can turn his back on Bobby and Jack Kennedy's civil-rights legacy and deny children a shot at a decent education.[28]

The House passes a $10 million private schools voucher bill for the District.[29] It is an amendment to the FY 2004 D.C. Appropriations bill (H.R. 2765), modeled after the D.C. Parental Choice Incentive Act (H.R. 2556). It grants low-income children in the District scholarships of up to $7,500.

The National Black Family Empowerment Agenda calls the voucher movement "phony" and a "conspiracy," saying it was "hatched" by the same "rich, racist, right wing foundation that funded Charles Murray's infamous book, *The Bell Curve.*" It

---

[26] Archibald, George. "D.C. Vouchers on Track in House," *Washington Times,* September 3, 2003.
[27] Ibid.
[28] "Kennedy = Maddox," *AtlanticBlog.com,* September 6, 2003.
< http://www.atlanticblog.com/archives/001102.html >
[29] Ford, Glen and Peter Gamble, "Right-funded Black Leadership Ascending D.C. Voucher Passage Is Huge Defeat," *NBFEA.com,* Sept. 28, 2003.
< http://www.nbfea.com/NEWS/news03/education/Voucher_Passage.html >

says that the Right bought Mayor Williams' support and calls Walden Ford a professional front for the Right.[30]

The *Common Denominator* (Washington's self-described "independent hometown newspaper") questions the source of funding for D.C. Parents for School Choice[31] and later publishes a photograph of Walden Ford's home along with her address.

Vouchers are criticized as primarily a ploy by the Christian Right to get money for religious schools. The issue divides black Democrats in D.C.[32]

Democrats complain that ads airing in Louisiana about Landrieu are actually attempts at suppressing black voter turnout and confusing black voters. They argue that the ads aren't actually on behalf of the D.C. Parents for School Choice but instead are tools of the GOP. Walden Ford says that the money for the campaign comes from Indianapolis insurance executive Pat Rooney. Democrats point out that Rooney is a major GOP financial supporter who moved his insurance agency out of Louisiana rather than follow state law restricting how much he could raise policy rates, and he was involved in a school choice coalition that violated Wisconsin's state campaign finance laws in 1997 in a state supreme court race.[33]

---

[30] Ibid.

[31] Sinzinger, Kathryn. "Who's Behind D.C.'s Pro-Voucher Group?" *Common Denominator,* October 6, 2003.
< http://www.thecommondenominator.com/100603_news1.html >

[32] Magnusson, Paul. "The Split Over School Vouchers," *Business Week Online,* October 13, 2003.
< http://www.businessweek.com/magazine/content/03_41/b3853127_mz02 1.htm >

[33] Hill, John. "Democrats Cry Foul about Black Radio Ad," *Town Talk,* November 13, 2003. < http://www.thetowntalk.com/html/2F45C88F-10CB-43A6-A3E3-816215C8F703.shtml >

The House approves a school voucher program for D.C. public schools as part of the FY2004 omnibus appropriations bill, giving a total of $40 million for D.C. parents, students, and schools. Of that amount, $13 million goes to school choice scholarship vouchers, $13 million goes to charter schools, $13 million to public schools for teacher training/recruitment and improving student achievement, and the final $1 million is for administration.[34] It is one of the closest votes of the year, passing 209–208.[35]

2004   **Despite a stall** earlier in the month, on January 22, the Senate approves the $14 million voucher program as part of the 2004 budget (Consolidated Appropriations Act of 2004). At least 1,700 low-income District children will be able to participate, each receiving grants of up to $7,500.[36] Although opponents had kept the measure from passing for four months, when the Majority Leader Bill Frist (R-Tenn.) and Senate Appropriations Committee chair Ted Stevens (R-Alaska) rolled the District measure into a catch-all federal spending bill, opponents passed the measure rather than risk a government shutdown.[37]

"We're free at last. After years of struggle, low-income D.C. families will finally be liberated from failing schools. For the first

---

[34] Hunter, Melanie. "House Approves DC School Voucher Program," *Cybercast News Service,* December 8, 2003.
< http://www.cnsnews.com/ViewPolitics.asp?Page=Politics/archive/200.../POL20031209a.htm >

[35] Hsu, Spencer S. "How Vouchers Came to D.C.," *Education Next,* Fall 2004.
< http://www.educationnext.org/20044/44.html >

[36] Hsu, Spencer S. and Justin Blum. "D.C. School Vouchers Win Final Approval," *Washington Post,* January 23, 2004.

[37] Hsu, Spencer S. "How Vouchers Came to D.C.," *Education Next,* Fall 2004.
< http://www.educationnext.org/20044/44.html >

time, we have real hope of closing the education gap between rich and poor. " –Virginia Walden Ford[38]

D.C. Parents for School Choice provides the Washington Scholarship Fund, which has been chosen to administer the scholarship program, with names of more than 1,400 families representing 3,000 students who are interested in the voucher program.[39]

The Heritage Foundation presents Walden Ford with its Salvatori Prize in American Citizenship for her leadership in the local battle to provide private school vouchers for students.[40]

The Archdiocese of Washington seeks more money to close an estimated $2 million gap created by costs related to the voucher program. They seek to amend the voucher law and get federal funds to pay for startup costs but are denied. They then turn to the private sector.[41]

2005   **The bill authorized a five-year pilot program** and necessitates a Congressional vote for continued funding each year. At this writing, the D.C. voucher program is in its second year.

---

[38] Strode, Tom. "Senate Approves D.C. Vouchers, Federal Ban on Human Patents," *BP News*, January 23, 2004.
< http://www.bpnews.net/bpnews.asp?ID = 17497 >
[39] "One Verdict on Vouchers," *The Washington Post*, April 21, 2004.
< http://www.washingtonpost.com/wp-dyn/articles/A29231-2004Apr20.html >
[40] "Ed Meese Drafted for Third-Party Ticket," News Release, May 2, 2004.
< http://forums.greenbaynewschron.com/read.php?f=2&i=53544&t=53510 >
[41] Hsu, Spencer S. "Church Seeks Help on Vouchers: Archdi8ocese Says Federal Program for D.C. Students Falls $2 Million Short," *The Washington Post*, May 6, 2004.

The D.C. Campaign for School Choice

	Key Supporters	*Key Opponents*
Organizations	D.C. Parents for School Choice, Fight for Children, the Cato Institute, the American Education Reform Council, Center for Educational Reform, Black Alliance for Educational Options, Institute for Justice	Teachers' unions, public education association, People for the American Way, Leadership Conference on Civil Rights, several Jewish organizations, National Education Association, National PTA
Financial Backing	Joseph E. Robert, Jr. (D.C. real estate mogul), J. Patrick Rooney (Golden Rule Insurance Co.), Richard M. and Betsy DeVos, Jr. (founders of Amway Corp.), Richard Sharp (Circuit City)	
Washington, D.C. City Officials	Mayor Anthony Williams, Council member Kevin Chavous, school board president Peggy Cooper Cafritz	
Members of Congress	Sen. Dianne Feinstein, Sen. Bill Frist, Sen. Judd Gregg, Rep. Tom Davis, Rep. John Boehner, Rep. Jeff Flake	Rep. Eleanor Holmes Norton, Sen. Ted Kennedy, Sen. Arlen Specter, Sen. Mary Landrieu

Editors' Opinions	*Washington Post, Wall St. Journal*	*Black Commentator*
Federal Government	President George W. Bush; former Education Secretary Rod Paige; Bush's senior congressional lobbyist, David W. Hobbs; former Labor Secretary Robert Reich	President Bill Clinton
People Noted for Switching Sides	Mayor Anthony Williams, Sen. Dianne Feinstein, Kevin Chavous, Peggy Cooper Cafritz	Sen. Arlen Specter, Sen. Mary Landrieu

Appendix E
The Legislation That Passed

Following is the full text of the three-sector bill accepted by the U.S. Congress and signed by President George W. Bush in January 2004. It allocated $14 million each to vouchers (private school scholarships), public schools, and charter schools. The D.C. School Choice Incentive Act was authorized for five years and funds were appropriated for 2004, with each of the four remaining years to be appropriated.

LEGISLATION

TITLE III—DC SCHOOL CHOICE INCENTIVE ACT OF 2003

SEC. 301. SHORT TITLE

This title may be cited as the "DC School Choice Incentive Act of 2003."

SEC. 302. FINDINGS

The Congress finds the following:

(1) Parents are best equipped to make decisions for their children, including the educational setting that will best serve the interests and educational needs of their child.

(2) For many parents in the District of Columbia, public school choice provided for under the No Child Left Behind Act of 2001 as well as under other public school choice programs, is inadequate due to capacity constraints. Available educational alternatives to the public schools are insufficient and more educational options are needed. In particular, funds are needed to assist low-income parents to exercise choice among enhanced public opportunities and private educational environments, whether religious or nonreligious. Therefore, in keeping with the spirit of the No Child Left Behind Act of 2001, school choice options, in addition to those already available to parents in the District of

Columbia (such as magnet and charter schools and open enrollment schools) should be made available to those parents.

(3) In the most recent mathematics assessment on the National Assessment of Educational Progress (NAEP), administered in 2000, a lower percentage of 4th-grade students in the District of Columbia demonstrated proficiency than was the case for any State. Seventy-six percent of the District of Columbia fourth-graders scored at the "below basic" level and of the 8th-grade students in the District of Columbia, only 6 percent of the students tested at the proficient or advanced levels, and 77 percent were below basic. In the most recent NAEP reading assessment, in 1998, only 10 percent of the District of Columbia fourth-graders could read proficiently, while 72 percent were below basic. At the 8th-grade level, 12 percent were proficient or advanced and 56 percent were below basic.

(4) A program enacted for the valid secular purpose of providing educational assistance to low-income children in a demonstrably failing public school system is constitutional under *Zelman v. Simmons-Harris*, 536 U.S. 639 (2002), if it is neutral with respect to religion and provides assistance to a broad class of citizens who direct government aid to religious and secular schools solely as a result of their genuine and independent private choices.

(5) The Mayor of the District of Columbia, the Chairman of the Education Committee of the City Council of the District of Columbia, and the President of the District of Columbia Board of Education support this title.

(6) This title provides additional money for the District of Columbia public schools and therefore money for scholarships is not being taken out of money that would otherwise go to the District of Columbia public schools.

(7) This title creates a 5-year program tailored to the current needs and particular circumstances of low-income children in District of Columbia schools. This title does not establish parameters or requirements for other school choice programs.

SEC. 303. PURPOSE

The purpose of this title is to provide low-income parents residing in the District of Columbia, particularly parents of students who attend elementary schools or secondary schools identified for improvement, corrective action, or restructuring under section 1116 of the Elementary and Secondary Education Act of 1965 (20 U.S.C. 6316), with expanded opportunities for enrolling their children in higher-performing schools in the District of Columbia.

SEC. 304. GENERAL AUTHORITY

(a) AUTHORITY- From funds appropriated to carry out this title, the Secretary shall award grants on a competitive basis to eligible entities with approved applications under section 305 to carry out activities to provide eligible students with expanded school choice opportunities. The Secretary may award a single grant or multiple grants, depending on the quality of applications submitted and the priorities of this title.

(b) DURATION OF GRANTS- The Secretary may make grants under this section for a period of not more than 5 years.

(c) MEMORANDUM OF UNDERSTANDING- The Secretary and the Mayor of the District of Columbia shall enter into a memorandum of understanding, as described in the statement of the managers, regarding the design of, selection of eligible entities to receive grants under, and implementation of, a program assisted under this title.

SEC. 305. APPLICATIONS

(a) IN GENERAL- In order to receive a grant under this title, an eligible entity shall submit an application to the Secretary at such time, in such manner, and accompanied by such information as the Secretary may require.

(b) CONTENTS- The Secretary may not approve the request of an eligible entity for a grant under this title unless the entity's application includes--

(1) a detailed description of--

(A) how the entity will address the priorities described in section 306;

(B) how the entity will ensure that if more eligible students seek admission in the program than the program can accommodate, eligible students are selected for admission through a random selection process which gives weight to the priorities described in section 306;

(C) how the entity will ensure that if more participating eligible students seek admission to a participating school than the school can accommodate, participating eligible students are selected for admission through a random selection process;

(D) how the entity will notify parents of eligible students of the expanded choice opportunities and how the entity will ensure that parents receive sufficient information about their options to allow the parents to make informed decisions;

(E) the activities that the entity will carry out to provide parents of eligible students with expanded choice opportunities through the awarding of scholarships under section 307(a);

(F) how the entity will determine the amount that will be provided to parents for the tuition, fees, and transportation expenses, if any;

(G) how the entity will seek out private elementary schools and secondary schools in the District of Columbia to participate in the program, and will ensure that participating schools will meet the applicable requirements of this title and provide the information needed for the entity to meet the reporting requirements of this title;

(H) how the entity will ensure that participating schools are financially responsible and will use the funds received under this title effectively;

(I) how the entity will address the renewal of scholarships to participating eligible students, including continued eligibility; and

(J) how the entity will ensure that a majority of its voting board members or governing organization are residents of the District of Columbia; and

(2) an assurance that the entity will comply with all requests regarding any evaluation carried out under section 309.

SEC. 306. PRIORITIES

In awarding grants under this title, the Secretary shall give priority to applications from eligible entities who will most effectively--

(1) give priority to eligible students who, in the school year preceding the school year for which the eligible student is seeking a scholarship, attended an elementary school or secondary school identified for improvement, corrective action, or restructuring under section 1116 of the Elementary and Secondary Education Act of 1965 (20 U.S.C. 6316);

(2) target resources to students and families that lack the financial resources to take advantage of available educational options; and

(3) provide students and families with the widest range of educational options.

SEC. 307. USE OF FUNDS

(a) SCHOLARSHIPS-

(1) IN GENERAL- Subject to paragraphs (2) and (3), a grantee shall use the grant funds to provide eligible students with scholarships to pay the tuition, fees, and transportation expenses, if any, to enable them to attend the District of Columbia private elementary school or secondary school of their choice. Each grantee shall ensure that the amount of any tuition or fees charged by a school participating in the grantee's program under this title to an eligible student participating in the program does not exceed the amount of tuition or fees that the school customarily charges to students who do not participate in the program.

(2) PAYMENTS TO PARENTS- A grantee shall make scholarship payments under the program under this title to the parent of the eligible student participating in the program, in a manner which ensures that such payments will be used for the payment of tuition, fees, and transportation expenses (if any), in accordance with this title.

(3) AMOUNT OF ASSISTANCE-

(A) VARYING AMOUNTS PERMITTED- Subject to the other requirements of this section, a grantee may award scholarships in larger amounts to those eligible students with the greatest need.

(B) ANNUAL LIMIT ON AMOUNT- The amount of assistance provided to any eligible student by a grantee under a program under this title may not exceed $7,500 for any academic year.

(4) CONTINUATION OF SCHOLARSHIPS- Notwithstanding section 312(3)(B), an eligible entity receiving a grant under this title may award a scholarship, for the second or any succeeding year of an eligible student's participation in a program under this title, to a student who comes from a household whose income does not exceed 200 percent of the poverty line.

(b) ADMINISTRATIVE EXPENSES- A grantee may use not more than 3 percent of the amount provided under the grant each year for the administrative expenses of carrying out its program under this title during the year, including--

(1) determining the eligibility of students to participate;

(2) providing information about the program and the schools involved to parents of eligible students;

(3) selecting students to receive scholarships;

(4) determining the amount of scholarships and issuing the scholarships to eligible students;

(5) compiling and maintaining financial and programmatic records; and

(6) providing funds to assist parents in meeting expenses that might otherwise preclude the participation of their child in the program.

SEC. 308. NONDISCRIMINATION

(a) IN GENERAL- An eligible entity or a school participating in any program under this title shall not discriminate against program participants or applicants on the basis of race, color, national origin, religion, or sex.

(b) APPLICABILITY AND SINGLE SEX SCHOOLS, CLASSES, OR ACTIVITIES-

(1) IN GENERAL- Notwithstanding any other provision of law, the prohibition of sex discrimination in subsection (a) shall not apply to a participating school that is operated by, supervised by, controlled by, or connected to a

religious organization to the extent that the application of subsection (a) is inconsistent with the religious tenets or beliefs of the school.

(2) SINGLE SEX SCHOOLS, CLASSES, OR ACTIVITIES- Notwithstanding subsection (a) or any other provision of law, a parent may choose and a school may offer a single sex school, class, or activity.

(3) APPLICABILITY- For purposes of this title, the provisions of section 909 of the Education Amendments of 1972 (20 U.S.C. 1688) shall apply to this title as if section 909 of the Education Amendments of 1972 (20 U.S.C. 1688) were part of this title.

(c) CHILDREN WITH DISABILITIES- Nothing in this title may be construed to alter or modify the provisions of the Individuals with Disabilities Education Act.

(d) RELIGIOUSLY AFFILIATED SCHOOLS-

(1) IN GENERAL- Notwithstanding any other provision of law, a school participating in any program under this title that is operated by, supervised by, controlled by, or connected to, a religious organization may exercise its right in matters of employment consistent with title VII of the Civil Rights Act of 1964 (42 U.S.C. 2000e-1 et seq.), including the exemptions in such title.

(2) MAINTENANCE OF PURPOSE- Notwithstanding any other provision of law, funds made available under this title to eligible students that are received by a participating school, as a result of their parents' choice, shall not, consistent with the First Amendment of the United States Constitution, necessitate any change in the participating school's teaching mission, require any participating school to remove religious art, icons, scriptures, or other symbols, or preclude any participating school from retaining religious terms in its name, selecting its board members on a religious basis, or including religious references in its mission statements and other chartering or governing documents.

(e) RULE OF CONSTRUCTION- A scholarship (or any other form of support provided to parents of eligible students) under this title shall be considered assistance to the student and shall not be considered assistance to the school that enrolls the eligible student. The amount of any scholarship (or other form of support provided to parents of an eligible student) under this title shall not be treated as income of the parents for purposes of Federal tax laws or for determining eligibility for any other Federal program.

SEC. 309. EVALUATIONS

(a) IN GENERAL-

(1) DUTIES OF THE SECRETARY AND THE MAYOR- The Secretary and the Mayor of the District of Columbia shall jointly select an independent entity to evaluate annually the performance of students who received scholarships under the 5-year program under this title, and shall make the evaluations public in accordance with subsection (c).

(2) DUTIES OF THE SECRETARY- The Secretary, through a grant, contract, or cooperative agreement, shall--

(A) ensure that the evaluation is conducted using the strongest possible research design for determining the effectiveness of the programs funded under this title that addresses the issues described in paragraph (4); and

(B) disseminate information on the impact of the programs in increasing the student academic achievement of participating students, and on the impact of the programs on students and schools in the District of Columbia.

(3) DUTIES OF THE INDEPENDENT ENTITY- The independent entity shall--

(A) measure the academic achievement of all participating eligible students;

(B) use the same grade appropriate measurement every school year to assess participating eligible students as the measurement used by the District of Columbia Public Schools to assess District of Columbia Public School students in the first year of the program; and

(C) work with the eligible entities to ensure that the parents of each student who applies for a scholarship under this title (regardless of whether the student receives the scholarship) and the parents of each student participating in the scholarship program under this title, agree that the student will participate in the measurements given annually by the independent entity for the period for which the student applied for or received the scholarship, respectively.

(4) ISSUES TO BE EVALUATED- The issues to be evaluated include the following:

(A) A comparison of the academic achievement of participating eligible students in the measurements described in this section to the achievement of--

(i) students in the same grades in the District of Columbia public schools; and

(ii) the eligible students in the same grades in the District of Columbia public schools who sought to participate in the scholarship program but were not selected.

(B) The success of the programs in expanding choice options for parents.

(C) The reasons parents choose for their children to participate in the programs.

(D) A comparison of the retention rates, dropout rates, and (if appropriate) graduation and college admission rates, of students who participate in the programs funded under this title with the retention rates, dropout rates, and (if appropriate) graduation and college admission rates of students of similar backgrounds who do not participate in such programs.

(E) The impact of the program on students, and public elementary schools and secondary schools, in the District of Columbia.

(F) A comparison of the safety of the schools attended by students who participate in the programs and the schools attended by students who do not participate in the programs.

(G) Such other issues as the Secretary considers appropriate for inclusion in the evaluation.

(5) PROHIBITION- Personally identifiable information regarding the results of the measurements used for the evaluations may not be disclosed, except to the parents of the student to whom the information relates.

(b) REPORTS- The Secretary shall submit to the Committees on Appropriations, Education and the Workforce, and Government Reform of the House of Representatives and the Committees on Appropriations, Health, Education, Labor, and Pensions, and Governmental Affairs of the Senate--

(1) annual interim reports, not later than December 1 of each year for which a grant is made under this title, on the progress and preliminary results of the evaluation of the programs funded under this title; and

(2) a final report, not later than 1 year after the final year for which a grant is made under this title, on the results of the evaluation of the programs funded under this title.

(c) PUBLIC AVAILABILITY- All reports and underlying data gathered pursuant to this section shall be made available to the public upon request, in a timely manner following submission of the applicable report under subsection (b), except that personally identifiable information shall not be disclosed or made available to the public.

(d) LIMIT ON AMOUNT EXPENDED- The amount expended by the Secretary to carry out this section for any fiscal year may not exceed 3 percent of the total amount appropriated to carry out this title for the fiscal year.

SEC. 310. REPORTING REQUIREMENTS

(a) ACTIVITIES REPORTS- Each grantee receiving funds under this title during a year shall submit a report to the Secretary not later than July 30 of the following year regarding the activities carried out with the funds during the preceding year.

(b) ACHIEVEMENT REPORTS-

(1) IN GENERAL-In addition to the reports required under subsection (a), each grantee shall, not later than September 1 of the year during which the second academic year of the grantee's program is completed and each of the

next 2 years thereafter, submit a report to the Secretary regarding the data collected in the previous 2 academic years concerning-

(A) the academic achievement of students participating in the program;

(B) the graduation and college admission rates of students who participate in the program, where appropriate; and

(C) parental satisfaction with the program.

(2) PROHIBITING DISCLOSURE OF PERSONAL INFORMATION- No report under this subsection may contain any personally identifiable information.

(c) REPORTS TO PARENT-

(1) IN GENERAL-Each grantee shall ensure that each school participating in the grantee's program under this title during a year reports at least once during the year to the parents of each of the school's students who are participating in the program on-

(A) the student's academic achievement, as measured by a comparison with the aggregate academic achievement of other participating students at the student's school in the same grade or level, as appropriate, and the aggregate academic achievement of the student's peers at the student's school in the same grade or level, as appropriate; and

(B) the safety of the school, including the incidence of school violence, student suspensions, and student expulsions.

(2) PROHIBITING DISCLOSURE OF PERSONAL INFORMATION- No report under this subsection may contain any personally identifiable information, except as to the student who is the subject of the report to that student's parent.

(d) REPORT TO CONGRESS- The Secretary shall submit to the Committees on Appropriations, Education and the Workforce, and Government Reform of the House of Representatives and the Committees on Appropriations, Health, Education, Labor, and Pensions, and Governmental Affairs of the Senate an annual report on the findings of the reports submitted under subsections (a) and (b).

SEC. 311. OTHER REQUIREMENTS FOR PARTICIPATING SCHOOLS

(a) REQUESTS FOR DATA AND INFORMATION- Each school participating in a program funded under this title shall comply with all requests for data and information regarding evaluations conducted under section 309(a).

(b) RULES OF CONDUCT AND OTHER SCHOOL POLICIES- A participating school, including those described in section 308(d), may require eligible students to abide by any rules of conduct H. R. 2673-132 and other requirements applicable to all other students at the school.

SEC. 312. DEFINITIONS

As used in this title:

(1) ELEMENTARY SCHOOL- The term "elementary school" means an institutional day or residential school, including a public elementary charter school, that provides elementary education, as determined under District of Columbia law.

(2) ELIGIBLE ENTITY- The term "eligible entity" means any of the following:

(A) An educational entity of the District of Columbia Government.

(B) A nonprofit organization.

(C) A consortium of nonprofit organizations.

(3) ELIGIBLE STUDENT- The term "eligible student" means a student who-

(A) is a resident of the District of Columbia; and

(B) comes from a household whose income does not exceed 185 percent of the poverty line.

(4) PARENT- The term "parent" has the meaning given that term in section 9101 of the Elementary and Secondary Education Act of 1965 (20 U.S.C. 7801).

(5) POVERTY LINE- The term "poverty line" has the meaning given that term in section 9101 of the Elementary and Secondary Education Act of 1965 (20 U.S.C. 7801).

(6) SECONDARY SCHOOL- The term "secondary school" means an institutional day or residential school, including a public secondary charter school, as determined under District of Columbia law, except that the term does not include any education beyond grade 12.

(7) SECRETARY- The term "Secretary" means the Secretary of Education.

SEC. 313. AUTHORIZATION OF APPROPRIATIONS

There are authorized to be appropriated to carry out this title $14,000,000 for fiscal year 2004 and such sums as may be necessary for each of the 4 succeeding fiscal years.

Source: U.S. Department of Education, "Legislation, Regulations, and Guidance," http://www.ed.gov/programs/dcchoice/legislation.html
Website accessed 2/9/05

Acknowledgments

In working to create choices for parents and give the children the chances they need to succeed in the District, I met many wonderful and caring people along the way. It's a little distressing to sit down now and try to acknowledge them; for one thing, I know I'll mess up and leave out one or two of those who made the biggest difference, and for another, there are people I never met who made incredible contributions of time and heart that I never knew about. Nonetheless, I do feel lucky to have this opportunity to express my gratitude in print:

For the D.C. Parents for School Choice parent leaders, whose leadership, commitment, and devotion were awe inspiring.

For President George W. Bush; Secretary of Education Rod Paige; Under Secretary of Education Eugene Hickok; Assistant Deputy Secretary for Innovation and Improvement Nina Shokraii Rees; Mayor Anthony Williams; Councilmen David Catania and Kevin Chavous; School Board President Peggy Cooper Cafritz; Senators Gregg, Frist, DeWine, and Feinstein; Representatives Flake, Davis, and Boehner; and *all* of the members of Congress and their wonderful staffers who supported us because of their strong commitment to children.

For *all* the members of the D.C. Coalition who made up the rest of the puzzle.

For my husband, Earlston II, who quietly and gently supported me and calmed me when the fight got too ugly and too hard and I got too tired.

For my children, William, Michael (Nikki), Miashia (Abba), Earlston III, Aaron, Desmond, Nathan, and Nigel, who gave me the best reasons to continue to fight.

For my parents, Marion Virginia and William Harry Fowler, who taught us (Gail, Renee, Doris, Harrietta, and me) by example to stand up and fight for what's right.

For my twin, Harrietta, who patiently listened to my venting every night and never hung up on me, even when I went on and on for hours.

For Pat, Joe, Brian, and Ann Marie, who stood beside me and guided me through the toughest of times.

For all my friends at the Institute for Justice who gave me incredible advice and encouragement, especially Liz and Lisa.

For my dear friends, Phyllis Berry Myers and Casey Lartigue, who always believed.

And for Rev. Floyd Flake and Dr. Howard Fuller, who inspired me many years ago to go on this journey and to whom I am eternally grateful!

Printed in the United States
124957LV00001B/124-138/A